GASLIGHTING

Recover From Toxic Relationships and Break Free
and Recognize Manipulative

(How to Avoid the Gaslight Effect and Recovery
From Emotional and Narcissistic Abuse)

Jeffry Calderon

I0222732

Published By Simon Dough

Jeffry Calderon

All Rights Reserved

ISBN 978-1-77485-366-5

Legal & Disclaimer

The information contained in this book is not designed to replace or take the place of any form of medicine or professional medical advice. The information in this book has been provided for educational and entertainment purposes only.

The information contained in this book has been compiled from sources deemed reliable, and it is accurate to the best of the Author's knowledge; however, the Author cannot guarantee its accuracy and validity and cannot be held liable for any errors or omissions. Changes are periodically made to this book. You must consult your doctor or get professional medical advice before using any of the suggested remedies, techniques, or information in this book.

TABLE OF CONTENTS

Introduction

The practice of gaslighting can be found in both personal as well as professional relationships. in other instances, gaslighting is utilized for public officials to alter the opinions of specific people. Gaslighting is a type that is psychologically abusive. It can cause you to doubt whether you can discern reality accurately. It may cause you to think you did not believe you observed or hear what thought you heard. And you begin to question whether you are able to believe the information you're receiving through your senses. In itself, could cause you to start to believe that there is something wrong with you and you'll start to doubt your own sanity.

It doesn't matter if it's the context of a relationship between people (parent with child or between lovers) or in a professional relationship at work , or even within one community. Gaslighting is a form of abuse which could lead to health issues if the victim remains in this situation for an extended period of period of.

It doesn't matter if it is an intimate relationship or business relationship or between an official and people in the public, or some other place it is crucial that you are aware indications of whether you, or someone else you are aware may be the gaslighting victim. being aware is the initial step towards ending the negative circumstance. The first step in order to be free of gaslighting is to understand the meaning of gaslighting. It can be difficult to identify warning signs that indicate gaslighting because they alter the mind to the extent that after a lengthy time, the victim is unable to believe in their own thinking.

This book will explain in depth how to differentiate gaslighting from the normal way of doing things by shedding some light on the various kinds of gaslighting methods. The book also provides readers with the information on how to proceed if you are in this kind of negative circumstance.

Gaslighting as it is described extensively in the subsequent sections, refers to a method employed by narcissists to control people. Narcissists are self-centered and arrogant people with no compassion for other people. They are a part of their own world, and believe they are unique and exceptional. They always want the attention and praise of others.

Narcissists often employ gaslighting because a narcissist's objective is to confuse the victim in order to gain complete power over the victim. The narcissist accomplishes this goal by slowly creating doubt within the mind of the victim, and then, in the end the narcissist is in control of the victim's mind and does their will.

Alongside educating people of gaslighting, this book has the purpose of revealing the extent to the extent that narcissists employ gaslighting to use manipulating and abusing their victims physically and mentally. The authors expose the words that of narcissists along with the ways they employ to victimize victims. It's one thing understand what gaslighting means, but it's a different matter to understand how narcissists utilize gaslighting to abuse victims. It's a different way to understand the negative effects of gaslighting and protect yourself from them - or better yet, prevent the negative effects from happening initially.

In addition, they teach you how to safeguard yourself, and possibly even free yourself from the grip of a narcissist who is gaslighting you.

Chapter 1: What is Gaslighting?

So, before we start with the subject, let's discuss what gaslighting actually is. It's a practice that a lot of addicts enjoy doing and many people, once they realize the problem, would like to take action about. In this article, we'll discuss the basics of gaslighting and why it's essential to be aware of.

"Oh Hey, Come On You're Just Being Sensitive"

Have you heard these words before?

This is an instance of gaslighting. If you've ever been in an argument and they respond with "oh don't you think you're being a child/too sensitive/I've did not say that" You've witnessed firsthand what gaslighting can be.

Gaslighting is actually a psychological term, however it is a form of manipulation in which the individual who attempts to manipulate is trying to cause someone to think about their own reality, their perceived reality, as well as their recall.

This is more dangerous than you think you are aware of, it's true.

It's not just about having people question their own reality, however. Gaslighters will continue to engage in this behavior, in the hope of making you doubt the legitimacy of your own personal knowledge.

It's always a risky thing since it alters the reality you live in.

A Gaslight At The Core

Gaslighting is the act of making the person who you spoke to denies your words and makes you appear to be lying and forcing you to question your reality. It's risky every time because it makes you give up on your own reality.

The offenses are typically minor. Perhaps, for instance, you're disappointed that someone did not perform something. You tell them this and they respond, "you're just being sensitive I'd never do this." Maybe they wouldn't have done it once But what would happen if they do it continuously.

Have you felt frustrated and a bit depressed when you are confronted with your own reality as a result of being gaslighted? Each of us has our personal reality and perspective of the scenario. It could be that you see things in one way, while another person who is looking at it from a different way.

The most sensible response the situation is to speak it out and work through the issue together and realize that both of you are living in the same reality. However, manipulators don't be concerned about any other person's reality, only their own, therefore they'll take whatever measures are necessary to destroy the reality you live in.

As time passes, you'll begin to think about your life and intentions. That's precisely what the manipulator would like out of you. The intention is for you to be completely skeptical of yourself to put you in a situation in which you're unable to bargain on the terms you'd like in your life or even on your own terms. instead, you're distracted on making the right decisions and generally have damaged your health and well-being.

Gaslighting isn't just a matter of in relationships between abusive girlfriends or boyfriends evidently. Anyone can be gaslighted. Your mother could be able to gaslight you. Your coworkers might. Your asshole boss can. Sometimes, people do not even be aware that something is taking place.

It's even possible to say that politicians do this. There are numerous instances where people are able to confront Trump regarding his conduct and he'll quickly deny the facts, debunking it in the hope of manipulating.

However gaslighting is extremely risky. Most people aren't aware of the dangers that could have occurred and frequently they don't act on it until it's already too late.

We'll discuss how to avoid an abusive situation in which gaslighting is involved in the future however, in the meantime, I'd like you to know the meaning of gaslighting at its base, and the indications of it.

A Dynamic Power Dynamic

The reason that gaslighting takes place is due to the power. The person who is being controlled has enough influence that the person whom they are targeting is afraid to change the relationship or leave because the danger of the relationship is present. Also, there is the possibility of being perceived as less than you truly are by other people which is a major risk. If you're feeling like you're losing influence within a friendship, usually you're probably gaslighting.

Family and marriage therapists do often and frequently, many suffer from being accepted, as the manipulator is known to pull the price in this scenario. People who are the targets of being gaslighted will also modify their views so that there's not a conflict.

The people who are gaslighted may not know that they're doing something wrong.

This could be due to how they're raised , or similar reasons. It is likely that you will encounter people who are gaslighting unintentionally frequently. The person who is doing this has bad intention, but it could be their way of doing things.

After you've learned some basic facts about it Here are some crucial warning signs that you'll see.

Gaslighting Signs

Gaslighting signs are easy to grasp.

You notice something you aren't sure about or perhaps you don't like the idea. Let's say, for instance, that Sally observes that Joe is playing with girls. Sally shares with Joe what she thinks.

Joe can be a manipulator or maybe he's thinking that he's saying he's complimenting them. He tells her it's just a compliment, and to be less too sensitive and not stress about things.

Sally lives with this reality and Sally receives a message that basically she's not right and that she's right, and must forget about everything.

You aren't sure. He advises you not to be worried and not to be "sensitive" and to not panic and react too much. However, you start to notice that you're beginning to question this.

It occurs again. You ask yourself the same question after which Joe becomes more defensive, maybe becoming somewhat rude and snappy with you. At times, at this point, Sally may begin to be concerned about her own behavior, since it could be the case with a "gaslight tango" meaning you're beginning to subliminally be a bit concerned about yourself.

The solution is often diffused , if you are careful with communication and understanding the reason you're angry. For instance, Sally could talk to Joe and tell him her perspective. However, real manipulators might not be able to comprehend the situation and frequently, they could critique.

In an abusive relationship, the person who is being controlled is likely to begin to be smothered in the end, and their knowledge and perception is nothing.

It's easy to see his parents too. If you're from a strict and strict family, parents, then you've likely experienced the effects of being gaslighted. If there's a person in your family that is a bit critical and apprehensive, they are likely to critique because they believe it's "what's most beneficial" for them. However, they might not be saying that in a negative way however they are perceived as being sarcastic and rude.

Most people will make this mistake with the intention of"I'm trying to assist." But it's true the assistance isn't really aid, but rather an attempt to alter the reality you live in.

There are certain signs that you should be aware of to be able to tell whether or you're experiencing gaslighting. A few of the most important indicators to be aware of include:

* They are keeping information from you

* They obliterate your memories of an event.

* They stop or divert traffic to put the victim on a different route

* They'll trivialize the circumstances, your feelings will be likewise diluted.

* They remember and deny, meaning that they aren't able to remember what transpired, or refuse to acknowledge something that happened previously.

If you begin to observe the signs above, it is likely that the person who is gaslighting you. We'll look at the exact signs you'll notice as a person who's suffered from gaslighting in the future.

Gaslighters can start by saying something that's true and truthful, yet you're able to sense when they point to it out. This can trigger a panic and instantly draw you into their worldview. It's their way of allowing them to determine what you're facing, and how you're experiencing.

If, for instance, you work with a colleague who complains that you aren't working enough at work They could say the fact that you are exhausted due to the fact that you have changed birth control. This could be true. It's true that you might feel depressed as a result of medication changes or other factors and yet they might then claim that you aren't pulling your weight. It could be the case that it doesn't suggest that you aren't pulling your weight. They could simply be doing it to make themselves appear like a snob.

Gaslighting is a form of manipulation with the intention to place you under their wing. The cases range from complete negation of the circumstances which have occurred to engaging in actions that can confuse the victim. The idea for this came in the Patrick Hamilton play called Gaslight which was later adapted which was a play in which gas-powered light bulbs in the home are dimmed when the protagonist explores the bright attic in the night. The main character tells her wife that she's believing it's the case that lights inside the attic appear more bright and that the lights inside the house are dimmed. The technique has been used in the study of clinical conditions, as well as in the literature that deals with research along with political commentaries.

Then, is it a Mental Health Issue?

If you're experiencing gaslighting, it's not mental illness. However it may be a sign of something else and an indication of it.

But, people with different personality disorders such as narcissistic disorder and even an antisocial personality disorder could utilize gaslighting to others to alter their perceptions to align it with their own. Psychologists have observed that people with these kinds of disorders are prone to deny doing something , even though they have proof. That's right, they said that, but they're totally denial, which looks awful.

Most of the time, you will encounter these issues with narcissists more than anything else, because they enjoy attracting those who are still early in their relationship by playing the pity party and bullying me in to get what they desire. If you don't accept their truth, they become very angry. Sometimes they even take the step of being stalked or follow the individual they are blaming to discredit their reality completely.

the ones who gaslit other have relationships that are mostly superficial and keep their close friends away and only talk to them for a short amount of time. They may view their self in a distinct manner in comparison to those who know them. They often are able to isolate people they have close relationships with from their families and friends in order to prevent them from being from them.

The people who suffer from antisocial personality disorder can also be called sociopaths. It is a state where individuals aren't concerned about the right or wrong way to behave and tend to ignore the feelings others are feeling too. They frequently annoy and manipulate other people with their lack of awareness, and not feel any remorse for their actions.

If someone suffers from this phenomenon smacks down others it is likely that they do not want to hear what you say, and don't actually spend the time to grasp and establish the connection, instead they will keep manipulating and avoid speaking out while they alter the way you see things.

Narcissists can be a whole category of worms We'll get into this in the next chapter.

But it's important to realize that if you're anxious about getting gassed, the likelihood is that it is happening. If you're noticing that your self-confidence and reality is constantly slipping away, it's an indicator of something larger and an issue.

How do you avoid this from becoming worse? We'll explain how to deal with people like this in subsequent chapters. First let's discuss Narcissists and how they fit into the overall picture.

Chapter 2: The Mental Game, And How to Stay Away From It

Manipulation isn't a good choice, no matter the kind of form it takes. The use of mental manipulation is among the most harmful practices. In many cases, it is known as psychological manipulative. Many have had to deal with mental manipulation at some point throughout their lives, but, not all of us are aware of it. If you've never recognized it, then it is probable that there were negative effects on you as a result of it. If you do notice it, based on how the time it has been going on for, the consequences can be devastating.

The goal of mental manipulation is to alter the perception of other people by deceitful or subversive methods.

The manipulator is able to gain advantage by using these strategies most of the time, and most of the time it's in the direction of someone else.

This type of manipulation is used to exploit people emotionally to allow the narcissist to achieve the power. The psychological or mental manipulation of people is seen throughout the globe. From the workplace to families It is sad how often such a nature can be detected.

It is essential to realize that there is a distinction between influences from society which are healthy and manipulation of the mind. The majority of us are affected by the people we interact with. It's the compromises we make in the course connections. These compromises aren't manipulative, but they are well-thought out and accepted by the of the parties involved. Mental manipulation is quite different. It only benefits the person who is manipulating it, regardless of the negative effects it has on the other side. The power imbalance is deliberate. The agenda of the manipulator is possible because of the exploitation of their victims.

There are many different techniques that are frequently employed by people who want to influence someone else's thoughts. Knowing these tricks will help equip you to confront those who are trying to take advantage of you to gain their own advantage.

We'll go through a wide range of methods that mental manipulators can employ to control you , or find their method.

The first thing that a manipulator might use to gain control over you is for you to be in contact with them in a place that belongs to them. Involving in places which are believed as theirs grants them more power. It could be their home, car or even their workplace. These are places that they control and hold some kind of control. Feeling like they own the space is what gives them authority. They are aware that you won't have a feeling of ownership or familiarity, making it much easier for them to remain in control of any discussions being held.

Another thing a psychological manipulator might do is allow you to speak first. This might seem attractive at first, however it's actually an effective tactic to allow the manipulator to gain control. They'll allow you to speak to help them identify weaknesses and be able to discern the basic patterns of thinking. Salespeople often employ this tactic when trying to determine whether you are willing to take the offer they are offering. They typically will ask lots of general and probing questions. They will use these questions to understand your thought patterns and the way you behave. Then, they'll be able to identify you are good at and what your weaknesses might be, which allows them to offer you a deal that you cannot refuse. This strategy of asking questions to get the desired outcome can be used in your personal relationships as well as at work. It is evident almost everywhere.

The next thing a mentally manipulator can do to gain control over the situation or you is to deceive you about facts. They might lie or come up with excuses to take

21

you off balance. Psychological manipulators are extremely sly. They usually try to make their victim believe they're responsible for the problem themselves. They accomplish this by changing the facts. It's also quite likely that, if you're dealing with a mind manipulator, they'll withhold or alter key bits of information, either exaggerating them or understating them.

The fourth indication of mental manipulation is a tendency to overwhelm individuals with numbers or facts. Narcissists often present themselves with the appearance of experts on a range of areas. They attempt to take advantage of people by providing them with facts and evidence to support the claims they make. They usually discuss topics that the person they're discussing with isn't familiar with in order to prevent rebuttals.

This fourth sign is seen to occur in many different fields. It's commonplace when it comes to sales, financial issues negotiations, as well as conversations between professionals. In addition, it is observed in relationship or social disputes.

Because this method makes someone appear like an expert and makes them feel like they have authority over you.

It is much easier for the manipulator to persuade you to accept their agenda.Sometimes there isn't a definitive end to the game, it's just to let the manipulator believe that they are superior intellectually.

The next stage is mental manipulation. It can be carried out through extreme bureaucracy. Psychotic manipulators try to make use of procedures, paperwork legislation, committees, and laws to keep or maintain their power. This can make your life more complicated, and it can also be used to prevent you from seeking the truth. This helps the manipulator cover up their weaknesses, flaws and flaws. It also lets them avoid judgments from others.

Mental manipulators often employ the tone of their voice as well as the motive behind it to achieve control. They believe that a loud voice can cause people to submit to their demands. This is a rather brutal method of manipulation However, it's quite amazing how often it succeeds. A loud voice, when paired with a strong body language definitely makes an impression. A lot of people are hesitant to submit since these kinds of words are difficult to comprehend, and it's easier to lie down and listen to the words they're using.

Negativity is often employed by manipulators. They go so in the direction of dazzling people by displaying negativity.

This lets them make you fall away from your equilibrium and create an edge mentally. This can happen in many ways. An example of this is notifying you at the last minute they are not capable of holding up their side of the bargain. The way they communicate it in the last second is an indication and coming at you without warning will not provide you with enough time to plan an attack. You might even end up offering concessions to ensure that the manipulator continues doing the job they've agreed to perform.

Lack of notice gives an individual a short amount of chance to take an educated decision. This is a tactic used by a lot used by negotiators, salespeople, and manipulators. When you pressure people to take a choice through stating that it is a time-bound offer or there are consequences for not answering now, you give the person making the argument. They will be more easily fulfilled due to the stress caused by absence of time.

Manipulators are also known to cover up their humor and sarcasm. They'll make comments that are insensitive and attempt to make them appear as jokes. They know that these kinds of remarks will make you feel less than and your feeling of self-confidence is weakened.

They might make sarcastic remarks about a myriad of items, including your appearance and the condition of your electronic devices and your qualifications or even your experience. In an effort at making you feel guilty or appear unprofessional in the eyes of your peers They believe that they be superior to you.

Alongside humor and sarcasm manipulators are known for their tendency to judge and criticize people so that they feel unworthy. This isn't as subtle in the same way as hostile humor. We make this statement because if an manipulator chooses to take this route, they'll make fun of, marginalize or even dismiss you in public. They do this in order to keep their an image of superiority and to keep you feeling out of balance. If they create the perception that you are doing an issue, no matter how hard you try to correct it, you'll likely feeling inadequate or like you might never be perfect or in some way. If you are constantly focussed on with no solution it can be extremely damaging to self-esteem.

Another technique that mental manipulators use is to give people the silence treatment. If you attempt to contact someone by phone or SMS, any number of other means and they don't reply and gain control, they are able to do so. This is because they are aware that you are waiting for a response which they are unable to give.

The goal is to create doubt in your mind.

They make use of silence to gain leverage, but it really is a mind game they play with you.

The mental manipulators can also be adept at fooling people. Faking ignorance is among their most effective techniques. They make it appear that they do not know what you are looking for or what it is that you're asking. If they do this, is a common way for people to take on the job for themselves. Children are known to often do this in order to persuade their parents into taking on the task or chore for them, since they aren't actually wanting to complete the task. If adults do this the reason is usually as a way to cover up something or escape any obligation.

The third and final technique that emotional manipulators prefer to employ is commonly called guilt baiting. This happens when an individual is able to target another's weakness or vulnerability. This allows the manipulator to force someone to comply with their demands or requirements. This is usually done by blameing other people. In addition, if they recognize your weaknesses and weaknesses, they're likely to exploit these. It could be them making you feel like they are responsible for their happiness, or unhappiness.

The final tactic that the mental manipulators are known to employ is to make themselves look like victims. They'll embellish their personal problems to gain the attention of others. If the manipulator is playing the role of a victim, it reveals the positive nature of those they manipulate. People feel the need to aid others in need, and the person manipulating recognizes this. They could reap the benefits of their own will through making it seem sorry for them. You could make concessions that you wouldn't normally do in order to assist them in healing, without realizing that they are making a deal with you.

How to Prevent Mental Manipulation

We've looked at the various methods that the mentally manipulator uses against you, we would like to offer some tips to prevent it. Naturally, nobody wants to be controlled, and knowing the signs and decide how to respond will make sure that you don't be a victim. There are many forms of manipulation and psychological manipulations can be more difficult to detect than other types of manipulation. We hope that you'll be able to gain enough knowledge through this text to guarantee your protection from these dangerous motives.

One of the techniques that is used by the mind manipulator is denial of what they've said.

You can stop this by simply making notes. If you take notes in notebooks or on your smartphone, it will provide the evidence you need in the event that the subject is brought up. Certain phrases are noticeable in an argument with the person you are manipulating, and writing them down places some power back in your control. This is a simple step that can be difficult for the person who wants to control you, and it's likely that they will get defensive.

It is important to be cautious in the event that you choose to employ this technique. It is possible to tell your swindler that you're recording things due to experiencing a lack of memory, but that might not be effective. They are quite adept in recognizing things and changing them on you. It is possible that at the end you're the one who feels guilt or shame. If you're in a situation where you think you should note things down so that they don't get lost lateron, you might want to think about why the person is present in your life.

Another method you can take to make sure that a mind-controller doesn't gain control over you is to remain aware of how you feel. Mindfulness is the act of being aware of what's really happening within you. When manipulation is involved the majority of us end up feeling uneasy or uncomfortable.

You might be feeling guilty, defensive and even feeling ashamed. These feelings can be a sign that the person you're dealing with might have a motive to manipulate you. In addition, you might know you're not being a criminal, yet it seems like you're being manipulated. This is a good indicator of manipulative psychology. If you're aware enough to be able to spot these signs this can help you to avoid falling into the trap set for you by the agent.

Just listening is another excellent strategy when facing a manipulative mind. They will constantly try to make you agree with their viewpoint. As you pay attention, you may be able understand their viewpoint but it doesn't need you to accept it. Letting the manipulator to speak also give you an chance to consider the words they're using and how you can be able to balance your internal thoughts.

The manipulators usually have a simple desire to be heard, therefore listening can give them something they need as well as ensures your safety as you won't need to alter your viewpoint. It also provides you with insight into what drives the person you're working with. This can assist you in finding resolution not only in your present situation but also the future as well.

Your personal experience and your beliefs influence the way you see things. You can assist yourself in not be manipulated by staying determined when it comes to these matters. It is essential to maintain the understanding that your viewpoint is valuableand is also legitimate. If you have control over your perception and your position, it enables you to keep your eyes open and avoid allowing yourself to be sucked in. This is the case even when facing a manipulator with an opposing view. If you keep your own viewpoint instead of surrendering to the manipulator's perspective, you'll be able to hold onto your own beliefs. This will allow you to not be as overwhelmed by the words of the manipulator. Make sure to study your beliefs and don't be afraid request some time to reflect on the issue. This will help you define what your opinions are about the issue instead of being overwhelmed and then simply to agree.

Although some manipulations stem from malicious intent however, not every instance is. Most of the time, it is trying to convince you to alter your point of view so that it is in line with your own. Always be sure to let the person you're speaking to know that you understand what they're saying. It is easy to do this by rephrasing the words they used and then stating that you trust the intentions of their words are valid.

Most people don't know they're manipulating other people.

We all find it easy to justify our actions. If they believe you aren't understanding their reasoning or you are thinking that their intentions are negative, it may result in defensive words and actions. These could lead to arguments that can be resolved by just re-examining the things they have said and then confirming their convictions.

Being clear and consistent on any subject could assist you in avoiding manipulating. Even if your partner does not agree with your viewpoint be sure to stay solid in your position unless you truly believe in what they have to say. If not however, you must be willing to with them. This could not go down nicely with the manipulator however, they'll have agree to it as long as they remain firm on the issue.

When you do the above actions you're giving yourself the ability to be able to resist manipulative behavior. These are just some of the numerous strategies that can be used to aren't manipulated. Be aware that trying to remain close friends or even with a manipulator will fail regardless of what tactics you use. Certain people aren't going to let one of these methods to happen, so you should get yourself from the problematic situation that manipulators may create.

Chapter 3: The Likely Victims

A lot of people mistakenly believe that those who suffer from gaslighting are always weak and vulnerable. It's not uncommon for people to believe that victims typically comprise mothers who stay at home and rely entirely of their wives for their needs, males who are at a loss over their wives' professions women who want to marry because they're not getting younger, or guys who are enthralled by women and are willing to accept all treatment. A relationship in which there is a lopsided power structure is a prime target for abuse psychologically. You can also be extremely successful and still be vulnerable to gaslighting. You might have a degree in engineering, successful medical professional, or an influential public figure, and yet endure emotional abuse.

A lot of individuals have an image of the ideal romantic partner that is heavily influenced by media, and so they treat their relationships by setting unrealistic goals and creating a list of traits. Their idea of the "ideal spouse" is someone with an excellent personality. They're looking for someone with a keen charismatic personality who is able to be engaging in lively conversations. The ideal partner must have an outstanding career track record and financial security, in addition to other attributes.

The issue of a person determined to control their companion by deliberately causing doubts in them could quickly master the art of putting on the appearance of these qualities to win their position. Once they've made their partner's heart, they may begin to alter their view of reality. This means that the primary motive for gaslighters is to build an effective rapport with or create confidence in potential victims, before causing the illusion of confusion.

This means that no matter how secure or successful the person may be they could be the victim of being gaslighted if they exhibit one or more of these characteristics:

*Conscientiousness - those who go to the extreme to do the right thing , because they are morally upright that they can trust easily and are reliable.

*Agree - people who generally want to get along with all people and would like to avoid conflicts, particularly with people who have close relationships with them.

Naturally, people who are insecure can be easy targets for gaslighters. However, during this section, I'm going to demonstrate how successful as well-educated, confident and ambitious individuals can be passive victims of emotional abusers. To accomplish this we'll compare typical characteristics of victims with some personality types within the Enneagram personality type system. Check to see what you connect with one of the traits listed below.

Codependents

People who are dependent rely heavily on fixing other people to feel satisfied with themselves. Their self-esteem is based on external influences that include making other people satisfied. They are responsible for the lives of others who suffer from physical or emotional health problems or suffer from behavioral issues like alcoholics and addicts. However, they only help to exacerbate (or facilitate) the conditions of addicts or those who are sick. Instead of a change the person who is addicted or an codependent suffers from their health, addiction, recklessness and insanity.

Here are some characteristics that make codependents easy targets for psycho-abusers.

An Urgent Need to Impact Others

Codependents aren't sure when to stop their efforts to influence others. While it's laudable to desire to help others behave in a positive way, it's essential to recognize that there's nothing that you can do to help people who don't want to change. The codependents who have a relationship with an abusive partner longer than they should because they believe that the person they are causing harm is going to change in the future, and it's their duty to ensure this happen sooner rather than later. It's similar to the "Reformer" persona who is entrusted with the responsibility of doing things right at all cost. In this case their self-worth is closely tied to the obligation to make people take the right actions. Gaslighters love it having their victims argue with them on what's proper and not. They don't know this, and get caught in this trap quickly.

Assistance When It's Not Necessary

Most often, codependents behave in the same way as those with the Helper personality. They will offer assistance even when others do not need their assistance. They are doing this because they think they can only improve their self-esteem is to offer assistance to other people. The emotional abusers may take advantage of this characteristic and lighten the mood of their codependent companion until every aid they provide appears inadequate. If the codependent partner is still convinced that their efforts aren't adequate the gaslighter has succeeded.

A tendency to be Extremely Self-Sacrificing

One of the biggest drawbacks of codependents is their desire to give up their selfless love to the level of hurting others. Maybe this is described in the sentence, "I'm going to love you even if it hurts my own self!" It is commendable to commit towards your loved ones, particularly those that are intimate. However, when your relationship turns into a source of hurt and pain the best thing should be to break it up and call the relationship off. If a narcissist believes that they are in the midst of an intimate partner who is apathetic will be just too content to keep committing abuse.

Empaths

The question of whether empaths are psychic as well or not will be a matter that will be the subject of a separate discussion. Empaths, as defined in this book, are people who have an extra level of empathy. They are able to feel others' suffering as if it were their own. Empaths don't have to work hard to be in the shoes of another. This ability, which could be good but can expose them to abuse of the emotional. Here's why.

They are unable to establish personal boundaries

The main aim of a narcissist or psychological abuser is get the control of their victims. Anyone who seems to be having a hard time making and setting boundaries for themselves is an ideal sign of the gaslighter. Lack of personal boundaries implies that the empath could be controlled and easily manipulated. If you are unable to be able to say no, and you are not willing to do it, you're an absolute gaslighter's delight.

They have a difficult time managing their inner critic

It's relatively simple for an empath to be guilt-ridden. A single harsh word and they'll spend the entire night pondering how insufficient they've been to be able to receive such negative criticism.

A person whose primary self-talk is based on statements like "How can I be so cruel and stupid?" "I'm not helping enough." "I am an irritant to my spouse," "I am not compassionate enough." "What could be wrong? Why am I so sensitive?" and so on cannot perceive reality as it really is. Their own perceptions of themselves block an accurate view of the events that could be taking place in the world around them.

Compassion is usually directed towards others Instead of Oneself

It's a lot simpler for empaths in general to be compassionate towards others than it is to cultivate self-compassion. They generally treat others as if they were friends, but they find it difficult to extend the same kind of treatment to them. They prefer to believe others' judgments more that their own. This can cause them to dismiss their thoughts, feelings and experiences to the benefit of another , especially when they show an act of self-control or has power.

They have a Big Heart

Being a person with a heart of gold is a great thing, unless people aren't considerate of you or even use them. People with a heart condition often struggle to distinguish their own feelings from the feelings of other people. They tend to accept the feelings and opinions of everyone else around them. People who are negative find this characteristic very attractive since they are able to take on the emotions of others and ride them for an extremely long duration.

The "Peacemakers"

Peacemakers are people who has a calm and relaxed personality. They tend to be peaceful people who stay clear of conflicts in any way they can. Peacemakers are extremely flexible and patient. It is a huge amount of effort for a peacemaker to let up on one they cherish. The general attitude they have towards life is typically a positive one, which is the reason they believe that everything will be good.

Peacemakers face a problem in they possess a strong dislike of being apart from those they cherish or think are important to their lives. Their sense of security appears to be derived from living harmonious with others. The fear of being in a group can make them stay in a relationship that is abusive for longer than they ought to. The way it manifests.

Extreme Modesty

The typical peacemaker is shy away from taking credit or granting credit for something notable. Even when they are praised by others but they dismiss it or dismiss their own opinion. They usually value others' opinions over their own. This is the perfect way for the person who is emotionally abusive to control the peacemaker and remain fully in control of the relationship.

Playing Second-Fiddle

Due to their excessive modesty, peacemakers tend to be a mirror for other people or to identify with them. They prefer to step back from the spotlight and let others to direction. They prefer to offer assistance to those around them rather than enlist the support of others. This insufficiency can keep them apathetic to those who push in opposition to their true desires. Instead of letting go and letting go, they'll hold on to their relationship, hoping they know what's most beneficial for them. Their anxieties and opinions rest on the premise why should they rock the boat since it's more about peace than being right? However, peacemakers aren't fast enough to grasp the distinction that exists between peace supreme and being taken to the edge.

Problems in Making calls

Peacemakers face a lot of difficulty making difficult choices. Inertia resistance is a common problem for them. A peacemaker is aware of what is right to do. If they're in a relationship that is abusive they will be able to recognize the problem and understand exactly what they must take action. However, taking the steps needed to make changes is not easy for them as they're not sure what to expect. They're a classic type of person who believes in hope but not actually. "Let I give this a second opportunity," usually keeps them longer in a tense relationship. The reluctance of them to let the bull out by the horns may lead to psychological abuse since they are put off from acting earlier.

The possibility of withdrawing

Instead of confronting other people and putting themselves in danger peacemakers prefer to retreat to the "protective" shelters, which are peaceful tranquility. They appear to be insecure and struggle to be assertive. These are two characteristics that draw people who are narcissists. When they don't want to make their opinions visible and their voice heard, they prefer to remain silent. They do not just avoid external conflict, they take every step to avoid internal conflicts as well. The problem with this type of mentality is that, in an effort to drown out their own voice, they are at risk of psychological issues, such as depression. They can also take up emotional eating or drugs, or even lying in front of the television to escape inner turmoil and to numb negative emotions.

The "Loyalist"

In the end, the majority of people who suffer from emotional abuse have the traits of a 'loyalist' type personality. One who is always looking for external structures that give them a sense direction is likely to be a victim of gaslighting, as well as other types that involve emotional violence. Structures are a great thing as it gives stability and direction. However, a loyalist finds it difficult to design frameworks for themselves. They prefer to have someone else provide them with a structure which is why they are vulnerable to abuse psychologically.

Additionally, many people who have low confidence in themselves and their self-esteem have this trait. They feel a greater fear of being vulnerable and insecure and search for help and assistance from nearly anyone who could provide guidance. Narcissists can take advantage of those with a loyalist personality and then take advantage of their vulnerability and insecurity.

Bottom Line

You might not be classified as an empath, a codependent or a Peacemaker Loyalist, or Helper which is fine. The classifications or the personalities aren't that important; they are just for clarity and not necessarily based on any rigid definitions. It is important to recognize some or all of these traits within your own. You might have several traits in each category, or only one characteristic. In any event, if you are able to identify yourself by this section, it is time to pay more focus on your relationships with other people and ask yourself some questions. Are you aware of someone close to you making a big deal of it? Do you often hear words "too delicate," "drama," "paranoid," or find yourself constantly apologizing for actions that aren't really your fault when you speak to an individual? Are you constantly speaking out against unfair treatment of other people, but you are still experiencing the same things in your own relationship because you're unable to confront the individual in the relationship? Are you feeling as if you're a failure, embarrassed or feeling very unworthy when you're with someone? Do you put in the effort trying to justify your partner's behavior?

If you've answered "yes" to any of the above questions, it's the perfect time to seek professional advice because you could be the person who has been gaslighted.

Chapter 4: The Way the Gaslighting Effects Your Mind

Gaslighting can be a very dangerous issue, since it could cause serious mental health problems for the person who is affected. Being a day-to-day living with self-doubt and confusion is enough to fuel the raging anger. Additionally, as a sufferer of constant gaslighting, the feelings of self-doubt and hopelessness could trigger depression, too. Alongside depression and anxiety It is not unusual for sufferers to develop unhealthy codependence as well as the post Traumatic Depression.

Gaslighting is clearly emotional abuse. Do not take it lightly Don't believe that simply that because you know the nature of it (or you've called your partner about it) that it is the end of this. It's not always the case. Anyone who will purposefully repeatedly cause you to doubt your memory and sanity is a scumbag who won't be able to change in a flash because you've exposed them to the wrong way to live.

Gaslighting is a shady manipulative and manipulative method that is so effective that it can negatively affect your mind. It makes you feel very unstable and incapable of thinking independently as clearly as you are accustomed to. In time, this anxiety becomes so overwhelming that you begin to turn at your abuser for clarity and direction. You're probably contemplating this Gaslighting isn't only a problem that occurs within interpersonal relationships. It is also a problem in the world of politics, by unscrupulous politicians who wish to ensure they have an even balance in their favor.

At first it seems like an ordinary dispute. You think there's nothing more to it. But, in order to recognize the issue for what it really is it is important to recognize that the perpetrator is known for lying every day and refusing to admit the truth even when there's evidence. They will also constantly engage in misleading you about the subject in question, and they are also prone to contradicting themselves.

The gaslighting of the mind and mental disorder

The first time gaslighting was seen clinically in the year 1969. The report found that in many instances, the sole reason that patients were in a mental institution was due to the fact that somebody (or someone) came up with a clever plan to make them appear mentally ill. This is known as gaslighting in its pure form, where the aim is to make one look and feel like a psychopath so that you will be completely eliminated from the situation. However, it's not always that extreme however. In the majority of cases people who abuse are engaged in gaslighting in order they can hold them under their control.

Sandra is a fantastic employee who excels at doing what she does. However, due to reasons unknown her boss makes a an effort to keep leaving the office during meetings. The memos never arrive at her. She's tried to talk to him to discuss it however he continues to wave her off with dismissiveness saying she's scared, and that she's likely losing the memos since she's not keeping her factual information in order.

Antoine discovers that he is the perpetual the victim to his father's emotional and verbal abuse. When he does speak about it his father tells the boy to "man up" because he's far oversensitive "like the girl."

In both cases it's clear that it's normal for victims to start to question their own view of reality. With this ongoing abuse, it's just the matter of time until Sandra thinks she's not as well-read as she used to be and Antoine believes in his father's assertion that he has to not be too sensitive.

What are the effects of Gaslighting

It's something to talk about gaslighting or narcissists, however it's a different matter to approach these issues from the perspective of the person you are. Let's examine the different negative effects that gaslighting could cause to your mental health and wellbeing. In the end, the victim has the same characteristics as a leopard who is unable to alter its spot. The primary aspect in the gaslighting game isn't the narcissistic victim however, but your own feelings.

In the majority of cases, when you're involved in a narcissistic or abusive relationship you'll be being constantly anxious, uneasy and concerned. You're feeling a sense despair and are in a state of helplessness. You're constantly walking around in a circle around the person you're with making excuses more often than you can remember, asking yourself whether you're correct, doubting your own abilities, and swathed in confusion. You realize that the activities you once enjoyed doing don't make you happy. No matter how you go about it you never feel confident enough. There is that unimaginable feeling of guilt and shame that shouldn't be yours to be a part of your neck. It's hard to feel mentally and emotionally exhausted.

Fighting doubtful feelings. The reason that your confidence is torn into pieces is because the person who is a narcissist starts their work by bringing themselves into the picture, and over time, the doubt oozes throughout every action you take. When you're trying to make connections with someone who's not able to focus or pay attention and who asks you questions that aren't easy about you, it's natural to start by asking yourself the same kinds of questions also. You believe that you're not capable of managing your own issues. In addition to adding more fuel to the fire you are feeling helpless in this situation, causing your self-doubt and self-doubt.

You've likely read blogs or books, which provide the grim reality: the narcissist not likely to change. It's inside your mind, however the heart is something else. Similar to the narcissist you start to believe in the fantasies of your own. "She can change her ways," You tell yourself and refuse to leave, trapped in the habit they've created within you. You may even be aware of when other people are being manipulated or gaslighted with their actions in their relationships. However, you insist that your relationship isn't the same. You try a variety of strategies however, you realise in time that you have no power. Your narcissist has all the cards and you cannot let go for any reason. The doubt seeps into the other areas in your daily life such as your family, career and friends.

Feeling not good enough. It's not surprising because we've been taught that when we're soaked in sweat, blood and tears, you can achieve anything. It's true in other areas of our lives but not the case with the self-centered narcissist. You are thinking, "If I could only improve, they'd be able to love me like they did at first." In your heart, you realize that you'll never be good enough to be loved by them.

It's as if they're always looking for your blunders and forgetting that these slip-ups should not be considered as part of the context of a healthy relationship. They don't notice any good thing you do and will quickly lay down the rules as well as make you feel guilty as soon as you step outside of the nebulous, always moving line that they keep within their head. If you keep trying and don't get noticed for what you did or not improve relationships with the demon and the more you begin to find yourself feeling inadequate and blame yourself. In extreme instances you may lose your self-identity. You don't have a idea of who you are. Be aware that that you're not enough. You're. You're being a victim of a narcissist. an endless abyss that is never filled regardless of the amount of your heart you offer.

In a sea of confusion. Today you're the center of interest. They shower you with sweet messages, gifts, praises and belly rubs, all the wonderful things. Tomorrow they're far and cold. They vanish without making contact. They wander off doing whatever they want and you've no clue as to where they are, or with whom they're. It's as if you're not even there. If it's good it's fantastic. If it's not then it's definitely not. In addition, the situation keeps moving from good to bad and back and forth between your two. Naturally, this makes you feel very uncertain regarding what your relationship and you are at! It's not your responsibility. Your narcissistic love is extremely inconsistent. It's just the nature of the beast.

It wouldn't have been as difficult If they'd been distant and cold from the beginning. You'd have been able to get away and go before there was a serious issue between the two of you. But this person can make you feel as if they understand the true essence of you. It's like your souls are entwined. They let you feel like that and tell you that it's the best thing that could ever happen to them. However, they'll try to keep you hidden from their friends who are in their lives and won't bother to be there to you when it truly matters.

The reason that you're confused is because an abuser is a devoid person who's attention is focused at what they consider to be the most fascinating or valuable at the moment. If that includes lavishing you with sweet things and gifts, they'll do it. If they find something else that's more appealing, they're gone. You're basically a target for the Narcissist. You're just an outlet for them. If they tell you they like your, they're not necessarily you they are referring to, but how they feel. Whatever "love" expressed is gone as soon as they discover something other than what gives them a sense of joy. If that isn't enough and boring, they're off to the next one. The only reason to be certain that the gaslighter is in love with you is because they've got charm and charisma throughout the day and more than enough to allow you to create something out of their sweet little quips. An endless stream of excuses. Alongside the self-doubt that affects your mind is the habit of apology, regardless of whether you need to or shouldn't. It is best to only apologize for a mistake. Also, you can use the word "sorry" when you observe that something else has caused people sad or disappointed to show compassion. For example, you could tell them, "I'm sorry for your loss." It's not really the fault of you, it simply makes it clear to the other person that you are concerned about their suffering.

If you're confronted by a gaslighter you'll notice the phrase "I'm sorry" is the new song you're hearing. It's easy to make them feel disappointed because they're entitled and want to keep people in the loop. You'll start to apologize for everything that you do, fuelled by your doubts. You will repeat, "I'm sorry... I'm sorry ..." because you've realized that no matter how you act you'll never be able give your partner the exact thing they desire.

Anxiety, sadness depression, anxiety and sadness. In addition to feeling stressed and depressed because of the lack of support you feel in your relationship, but you are feeling this way because the gaslighter isn't someone who can share your feelings. You're constantly depressed and sad and you're not doing things you previously enjoyed and you're constantly feeling guilt, you feel unworthy and frequently withdraw from any social activities. It's hard for you to sleep and you develop poor eating habits too. When you're depressed you're not able to cope with the gaslighting appropriately. Your mind is broken at this moment.

Gaslighting can cause anxiety to the extreme. When you feel that you are unable to resolve your relationship or return it to normal regardless of how you try your anxiety grows and can eventually escalate to complete anxiety. You can feel your heart beating. It's difficult to breathe properly. You get dizzy spells. The feeling is overwhelming that something awful is likely to happen very soon.

Fortunately, both anxiety and depression can be managed. All you need to do is consult an experienced psychotherapist who will assist you in overcoming the issues your feelings, provide you with useful tools to get past gaslighting and abuse and provide you with the necessary medications to improve your condition.

The learned helplessness. In time after you've had the option of enduring the same situations that you'd prefer to avoid, you realize that you're not able and often unwilling to act on your situation -- even though you've got the ability to stop it. This idea is known as "learned in helplessness" and was invented at the Pennsylvania University by Martin Seligman. It is learned that there's no way to fix the issue, and you continue to accept it. Even when you have the chance to get rid of it or put an end for it do not. This isn't your responsibility. You've been trained by the gaslighter that you should feel powerless.

Gaslighting can cause helplessness, increasing your chances of having to experience depression and depression and. If you've been the subject of gaslighting for a long period and you accept that this is the way things will be forever. You are numb to your life and don't bother to speak up against your abusive partner. You know that you are able to walk away but since you've been taught to keep things in order that they will improve but you don't. You believe that if you do your best and do your best, you will be able to create a positive relationship between you and your partner.

Loss of enjoyment. One thing that is common when people suffer from gaslighters is their disinterest in activities that normally give them joy. Perhaps you've noticed that since the time things started to go downhill in your relationship that you are a victim of abuse, you are no longer able to enjoy being with those you love to be with and you're no longer interested about the Taekwondo training that you were so excited about. Your life shifts between black and white and you no longer have any motivation to get involved in anything at all. If you could summarise all the emotions you feel in only two words What's the point? Because of the discontent that you feel about the relationship you are in, it is clear that you are unable to longer want to enjoy life's little pleasures. The discontent bleeds from the relationship to other areas that you live, so completely cease to care.

An overwhelming sense of shame. The most horrible, sad thing of shame is that it makes you make worse decisions. The person who is a gaslighter simply doesn't have the capacity to confront the guilt they feel inside, which leads them to make the worst decisions. If you attempt to make the person accountable, they'll react by screaming and then doing something even worse. What does it mean for you?

You'll know when you've committed something you ought to feel ashamed about. However, you accept it, learn from the experience and move on vowing to never repeat the same embarrassing behavior again. In other circumstances you may try to keep yourself off from others to avoid being judged or because guilt is eating away at you. It's similar to talking about how healthy your choices for food are when you realize that you sneaked out to the store at 2 am to purchase chocolaty bars (which you devoured in private obviously!)

Through the duration of your relationship with the gaslighter, it's easy to feel embarrassed as family and friends start to make a point that the way in which the way they treat you in a way that is unacceptable. It's possible that you feel embarrassed by the way you're treated and even though you're aware more about it, due to reasons that aren't clear, you continue accepting it. It's also a shame that you think that people are judging you for not continuing to live your life. The shame is felt from multiple different angles. When you realize it you're trying to avoid contact with people that could aid you in escaping. You get tired of telling others to make it appear that everything is in order for you, and with your partner who is a gaslighter. If you separate yourself from people who hold your best interests in mind You realize that you are more vulnerable to being gaslighted in the way they would like to do.

Mental and emotional exhaustion. Being engaged to one who is constantly smacking you in the face is exhausting. It's difficult to comprehend what's happening and you use up lots of mental energy trying to figure out what's going on with the person who promises to love you. You're exhausted emotionally because every day (even every hour) presents a new challenge. It's as if you're engaging in endless arguments. You're having constant conversations. It's not changing regardless of how sincere they seem when they say they'll strive to be better.

The fatigue dulls your mental abilities so that your performance in workplace or school isn't as good as it used to be. It also affects the effectiveness of your relationships , and can lead you further into isolation. In the end, the mental dangers of gaslighting are extremely real and can be very damaging to your life in every way.

Chapter 5: Understanding The Gaslighter

Gaslighters come with a variety of characteristics which are important to understand. The rundown in this section may appear to be too long or broad. The reason I'm breaking down the rundown isn't just to provide an academic definition of gaslighting that is so broad as to provide a better understanding of what gaslighting actually is, the method by which it is used, but to show how to recognize the signs.

There's a chance that you'll be thinking, "Well, that could be a representation of the differences between me and my sister sometimes but she's not gaslighting." What we're looking at are the designs. If the right characteristics are readily available and persistent in a person, chances are that you're dealing with gaslighters.

Therefore, we must begin painting our image.

Their Apologizes are Always Conditional

One of the most important things that people regularly observe about gaslighters is that they're experts in the "contingent expression of regret." That's right, when someone declares, "I'm sorry you feel like this." This isn't a friendly sentiment as the person saying it does not assume responsibility for his actions, but he's essentially influencing the person to feel seen through acknowledging your feelings. Gaslighters might apologize in the event they're trying to extort something from you. If they apologize or express regret, if you pay attention you'll realize that it's really a non-apologetic that they'll usually offer it because you asked for one or due to the reality that they're compelled by an official or middleman to behave what they are required to do.

They Make Use of Triangulation and Splitting

Gaslighters are the best strategies for controlling people, but two of their top choices are triangulation and dividing by creating a wedge between them and other people is a way to overwhelm and manage. Let's examine these two methods. Gaslighters find and split for the reasons that follow:

To put people against one another

To convince people to join them

To ensure a safe distance from the head-to head showdown

To ensure a safe separation from any obligation related to their actions

To spread your character

To spread falsehoods

To create chaos

Triangulation

Triangulation is a mental term for communicating with someone via other people. Instead of addressing someone legitimately gaslighters go to a friend or a friend or a relative, or a parent, to receive a message. Triangulation behavior ranges from correspondence--"I really want Sally to stop making calls at my house," hoping that someone will relay this message to Sally and even sly proclamations such as,

"Kindly advise Sally to stop calling me." Both are manipulative and circular.

Parting

Gaslighters are also known to set people against each other. This is called splitting. It provides them with a sense of control and intensity. It is possible to be a lie between a person and one another, claiming that a companion of common interest had made an unflattering comment about them.

Gaslighters are the most effective fomenters and troublemakers. They suffer a force-impact when they cause people to be frustrated and fighting each other. Gaslighters at this moment be able to watch calmly at the sidelines witnessing the exact battle they created.

Be aware of this basic rule If someone doesn't say something in a legitimate manner then you should be sure that what you're told about you was made by the person who said it isn't true.

Gaslighters know that separating and looking will draw you closer to them, and also separate them from the person they're setting you up against.

They Make Blatant attempts to curry favor

Gaslighters also have a knack for making people feel adulated. They'll make use of fake praise to obtain what they want from you. If you meet their needs then they'll shed their notion of excellence. Trust your gut. If the generosity appears limited or fake, be cautious.

They Are Expecting Special Treatment

Gaslighters think that traditional social norms, like respect, amiability and tolerance don't apply to their lives. They're not bound by the rules. For example, a gaslighter might expect that his partner be at home at a certain time and have dinner on the table after returning home. If the other person doesn't fulfill the obligation and the gaslighter becomes to be extremely angry and responds with anger.

They mistreat people with Little Power

You can tell a good amount about people by the way they treat a person with less power than they have. Take look at how someone is treated by the waiters in an establishment. Does she yell at the employee or does she ask favorably? What happens if a dish appears and it's not what the coffee shop had mentioned? Do they confidently but willingly ask for a change, or is she able to cause an uproar and shout at the employee? Disparaging the worker could be an effect of gaslighting.

Another indicator of gaslighting is how people behave towards or look at children or animals. There's a difference between not being interested in animals or children, as well as treating them with a snide attitude. Gaslighters can yell and focus on individuals or animals they perceive as "lesser."

There is a possibility gaslighters are prone to street outrage. They are aware of someone cutting off their limbs or not using the blinker in one attack. They're prepared to settle the issue and rectify the wrong "off-base" that was committed to them. This behavior puts various drivers and gaslighters' various passengers at risk.

They make use of your weaknesses to attack They Use Your Strengths Against

In most cases, you'll begin your relationship with someone who is feeling secure and security, so you'll do what any human being in what she believes is a healthy relationship will do: you share your thoughts and thoughts with the person. This is normal, common and is a solid way of creating a comfortable relationship. But, take note that the gaslighter is not likely to reveal the same amount of personal information about himself. In the end, the information you provide will soon be used against you in battles, and it becomes mental ammunition. For instance, the information you made to the gaslighter your uneasy relation with your sibling now being rebuffed as "No big surprise that we are fighting. Your sister isn't happy with too. You treat her the same as that you would treat me."

They will compare you with others

Gaslighters can also employ the concept of correlation to aid in making people feel uncomfortable and then gaining control. Guardians who gaslight frequently contrast their children with one another, and in hilarious and plain-faced ways. The guardian who gaslights typically is an "prodigy" as well as is a "substitute younger child." The former can't be blamed in any way, while the latter is unable to do wrong. This puts kin in opposition each other, and the rivalries usually extend to adulthood.

Your supervisor might ask, "For what reason wouldn't you be able create the same kind of work as Jane? Jane gets up at 8 every day. If she can do it, then so can you." It is possible to be at the wrong end of a relationship, apart from when it's to critique the "opposition." This means that gaslighters can encourage you towards other people, even if they are likely to make other people look horrible. In the end, you're not going to be able to do anything wrong regardless of how diligently you strive to fulfill the gaslighter's absurd expectations.

They are obsessed with their Performances

Gaslighters often gloat about the achievements they have created, such as the way they received an award for representative of the month at work. Don't worry about it because it was 15 years ago! They'll berate you if you don't react with enthusiasm and praise when they tell that they did indeed inform you the time the "dropped their microphone" on someone. Gaslighters place an absurd amount of importance on their accomplishments regardless of how arbitrary their accomplishments and skills might be.

They prefer to be with people who are awed by them

Friends who could speak out against gaslighters over their conduct do not belong in gaslighters' lives. Gaslighters only connect with people who put them in a religious setting and the way in which they think they have the right to be treated. They will feel that you are not appreciated any more and are not taking into consideration their views, they'll drop you.

They place you in a Double bind

Twofold ties can be a situation in which you are forced to choose between two tense options, or are presented with contradicting messages. As an example, if your unintentionally obnoxious spouse informs you that you need to lose weight, and then serves you various sweets at dinner. You're in a bleak situation. Gaslighters are known for putting people in emotional binds. Your vulnerability could be an indicator to them that they are in control over you.

They are obsessed with their Image

How do your gaslighters appear ugly! They'll pay back them. Gaslighters are focused on their appearance to others. They spend a significant amount of money in preparing items and spending a lot of time looking at their reflections. They might be steamed when you rub their hair or use some of their prep items. They are looking for perfection, and it's not easy to obtain. Some gaslighters even go not have to cover an operation to restore their appearance and other techniques to improve appearance.

They're Obsessed With Your Image

Gaslighters are not only in a position to be overly focused about their appearance They can also be very specific about what you appear like. Weight will generally be the main focus for gaslighters. They will smear their companions regarding their weight and clothing selections. Gaslighters buy clothes for their friends they believe to be as acceptable. The main message is that you're a bad person.

They deceive People

All games are played for gaslighters, and conning is an essential part that is part of.

Gaslighters must be aware of how much they could deceive you either sincerely or financially. They are also not as smart as they believe. They will openly talk about their scams. This is what frequently leads to their loss.

They create fear in others

Family members of a gaslighter might shield the gaslighter from those who decide to go at him for the conduct of his employees, or decide to stay clear of challenging the gaslighter. This is due to two primary reason: (1) The loved people have become familiar with the behavior of the gaslighter and believe that it is normal; and (2) they're attempting to protect themselves from appearing suspicious of the gaslighter. This is especially common in the children of gaslighters.

They're Not a Good Temper

Gaslighters believe their "owed" loyalty to others and because they have a fragile self-image and that any behavior is viewed as a gaslighter's fault, and often resultant in the victims. The danger of firearm violence is high with gaslighters due to their rages. The United States, 8.9 percent of the population have aggressive behavior and firearms (Swanson and co. 2015).

Gaslighters will from the beginning try to hide their anger to keep their facade of perfect. However they could maintain this fake appearance for so long. When you first witness the gaslighter disappear from the cover, it can be extremely frightening.

Discipline isn't a factor in their lives.

People with Cluster B character problems that are more prone to gaslighting and will generally possess a different neuron-terminating pattern as compared to others, when they are they are taught or rejected. They don't also value prizes in the same way that other people do (Gregory and co. 2015). This means the discipline and rewards will generally be less influential and can lead to gaslighters' generally likely towards "do whatever they think of doing" without worrying about the reaction from other people.

They are trained to practice "Psychological Empathy"

Gaslighters can appear to understand what you're feeling, but examine further and you'll find an almost mechanical look to their expressions of empathy. The responses they give seem to be prerecorded or standardized, but there is no real emotion behind their statements. Gaslighters are experts at using "intellectual compassion"and acting like they feel compassion, yet they don't feel it.

They deny personal responsibility

It's always someone else's problem. That is the mantra of gaslighters. Like we said before, people with the character issue is known as personality syntonic conduct. The result is that people who suffer from character issues feel that they're normal and everyone else is crazy. They believe their behavior is acceptable and that it addresses concerns that their conscience has. This is one of the reasons why people with issues with their character are difficult to deal with because they do not believe that there is anything wrong about their behavior or conduct.

They wear You down after a while

Gaslighters are betting on the chance that, with enough chance they could destabilize your spirit. They also anticipate that if they gradually expand their manipulative behavior they will make you the most infamous frog inside the pan. Therefore, they'll expand the temperature so slowly that you aren't aware that you're actually consuming your mind alive. In the beginning of the relationship you have with gaslighters it could be that things are fine, but and logical. But they're not. Gaslighters may still congratulate your every now and then. After that, the reactions begin to take over. What is the reason for this reversal between disdain and applause? Gaslighters recognize that disorder can weaken the mind. When you are vulnerable, you also become weak. At the point of the endof your relationship, you're taking on a lie that you never accepted at the beginning in your friendship.

They are prone to lying

If gaslighters get caught using the well-known "hand inside the container for treats" they'll look at you in a straight, unflinching manner and tell you that they didn't do anything like that. This makes you doubt your mental stability. I may not notice them doing this in all likelihood. That's what they want to see happen, which is to cause you to end up becoming more dependent on their perception of reality. They might even move things forward by revealing to you that they are losing your mind. The things they say to you by gaslighters are insignificant; they're constant deceivers. Therefore, it is best to pay attention to what gaslighters do, not the things they claim to be saying.

They're Terrible Teasers

Gaslighters are a pity. From the beginning the conversation is a matter of little details in the absence of from the rest of the group such as what your hair looks like or the way you articulate. This can then escalate the amount of their nagging you in front of your friends. If you say that their comments or behavior is causing you to be disturbed it is obvious that you're too delicate. It's not the same as merely normal family members prodding or playing games with friends. For gaslighters, it's an endless prodding. It has a stale quality in it. It is it is usually important, your requests to have it stop will go unnoticed.

Their Gratitudes Aren't Real

The gaslighter is skilled at giving "compliments," a portmanteau of affront and praise. There's anything like an actual commendation from gaslighters (or the narcissist). It's always a bit naive or uninvolved.

They show their emotions

Gaslighters might have their extremely own feelings of helplessness or actions that they do not know that they're planning their actions on someone else. For example, a gaslighter may declare that you are in need of a medication test, even though he own self, will be the one that is using.

They will isolate you

Gaslighters generally reveal to the person who they are that your family members can have negative consequences on you and that you do not seem to be happy when you're with people you truly love. They could also say that they won't join family events with you due to "Your family is making me feel awkward" or some other nebulous or unsubstantiated reason. A gaslighter may be relying on the chance that rather than telling your family members why you're attending an event with him, you'll end in a situation where you're not with him. The more successful the gaslighter is in isolating you, more vulnerable you will be to his influence.

They use "Flying Monkeys"

Gaslighters may try to communicate with your contacts through other people, especially when you decide to make the risky decision to stop communication.

These people are they're snooping around to transmit gaslighter's message.

They tell others that you Are Crazy

Gaslighters can create friction between you and other individuals in a variety of harsh ways. When you end your vocation with a gaslighting leader such as this colleagues may confess your boss that they were pondering what was going on and in light of the fact that their supervisor had instructed them to "proceed with care around this one." There's not a better way to destroy your reputation than to inform people that you're insane. People are currently viewing you as a delicate and unstable.

They don't keep their promises

For gaslighters, guarantees are made only to be broken. If gaslighters promise you something consider it an unfulfilled promise. In the event that the gaslighter is your boss, have these guarantees documented as hard copies.

Faithfulness is Required, but Not Reciprocally

Gaslighters demand total and unimaginative determination, but don't expect a commitment from gaslighters. Gaslighters can do anything to you, but God will be with you in the chance they believe that they've been a bit naughty. They'll turn your life into miserable.

They kick people when they Are Not Happy

It is not just satisfying by letting sleeping dogs rest after they've done their damage, but gaslighters also keep beating people who are lying on the ground. They experience a flush of satisfaction from watching other suffer. They get excited when they see someone else suffering as a result of their actions.

They are reluctant to admit the problems they've Created

Gaslighters might say they think you or the people who are around them, are naive and are a bit off base but in the end, they do not account for themselves, or taking responsibility for their actions. For instance, they may risk the lives of their colleagues because they do not adhere to workplace health and safety regulations. In the event that they confront managers about their infringements they argue that no one was actually hurt or was injured, and that they're not focusing on the right things. Then they are slammed by guardians when they are informed by their child's teacher that it's beneficial to will spend more time reading at home, and accordingly scold parents who are not responsible for their child's problems in reading, or blame teachers or schools of bringing the issue up.

They are Bait and Switch

The manager of your gaslighter stops at your desk and asks you if you've got just a few minutes to discuss a different task. You're energized, specifically due to the fact that this extra work could be an incentive to the manager to offer you an increase. When you meet with your supervisor and supervisor, you're told that you're involved in a new project because a different person was picked up. Now, you're assigned extra work with no remuneration. Before you are allowed to make questions, the supervisor announces to you that he's busy and closes the entrance behind you. This is a fantastic technique to control people by promising them something specific before turning the switch once they accept the promise.

Chapter 6: 30 words that Gaslighters love to use

Stuff Your Gaslighting Abuser Says

If there's one thing that I've learned from working with those who faced the challenge of gaslighters who are manipulative It's that invariably the perpetrators appear to have a few common phrases they've all used. It's like they've all attended Gaslight University or something. This is what your abuser will tell you:

1. This is only because you're insecure.

2. You're too sensitive!

3. Stop being paranoid.

4. It's not really a huge issue.

5. I thought I was joking!

6. You are too serious about things.

7. You're acting crazy right now.

8. You're somewhat crazy, aren't you?

9. It's just a matter of making everything up.

10. Stop being so hysterical!

11. Can you be more dramatic?

12. You're so ungrateful!

13. It's all in your head.

14. That has never happened.

15. You're lying. Everyone doesn't believe you. I don't believe in your lies.

16. If you've paid your attention.

17. We've talked about this before. Do you remember?

18. Aren't you thinking you're exaggerating?

19. If you've just listened.

20. You continue to jump to wrong conclusions.

21. The only person with whom I've ever had problems with.

22. I'm talking about, not arguing.

23. I understand exactly what you're thinking.

24. What is it that says about you that you believe?

25. The reason I don't criticize you is because I'm watching for you.

26. Don't take anything I'm saying so with a pinch of salt.

27. You have to improve in communicating.

28. Relax and calm down.

29. You're thinking too much about this. It's actually not that complicated.

30. What happens if you're wrong once more as you did the first time?

Consider the context you hear these words used to you. Did you mean sexuality? Family? Money? Are there habits either of you have? These phrases frequently pop up when conversation is focused on that.

It's a sad reality it is that for major of the time, the victim is female, while an narcissist who is gaslighting is an adult male. The reason for this division of genders and narcissism comes from the fact that the majority of women have been taught to be self-conscious and apologize when there's a problem or disagreement with partners. But men do not have this socialization.

Examples of Gaslighting

Scenario 1. Mark and Jeanine are two people who have been in a relationship for some time and are currently. At first, Jeanine never realized she was in a relationship with a narcissist who constantly criticized her when she was not around which made her look unpopular to her family and friends. Jeanine was puzzled for quite a while how her friends and family were not separating from her. A few days ago she had a heartfelt discussion with her sister's top acquaintance, Ruthie, who told her that the reason that everyone had a problem with her was that Mark had informed her that she was constantly abused by himverbally and physically.

And, Mark had the proof that he was even able to send himself email using Jeanine's account, splashing himself in hot water on occasion and sending pictures to her family to discover what fresh devastation Jeanine was allegedly causing him. In the meantime, every time they would appear they would see him as the loving, caring husband who made her friends and family resent her because of something she didn't do! Jeanine would beg her husband to talk to her often and complain about her declining relationships and friendships, and he would console her by telling her that it was just a figment of her imagination and that they cared for her and that she was just being a little paranoid.

Scenario 2. Amy was always in an extremely difficult relation with her mom Lucy. Her mother had hurt her in a brutal way as she grew up and every time they were at home. Lucy would force Amy sit in the bath while she poured scorching boiling hot water in the tub, causing pain to Amy severely. Lucy would tell Amy various grotesque things, including, "You're good for nothing, Amy. You only do cause damage to the world."

In the meantime, when other children are around, Lucy is the perfect mother. Then, we come to Amy becoming a mature adult. Amy chooses to talk to Lucy about her frequent assault and is able to do so. Amy is shocked by the reaction she receives by her mom. Lucy just says,

"None of that ever took place. It's just a matter of imagining things. You're an infant. Kids of that age are ignorant. You're no exception." However much Amy tried to convince her mother to acknowledge her actions, Lucy denied it all even going on about the matter. Amy determined to break up with her abusive mother and to never speak about the incident ever again, since it was evident she wasn't going to be able to get an apology from her mother for her abuse and neglect, or even an acknowledgement that it took place.

Chapter 7: Narcissism In Relationships: What can we do?

When narcissism is a symptom of the course of a relationship it can cause anxiety and even fear because the people who are narcissistic get hopelessly in love far beyond what we'd expect. But its care-giving component creates "a rope" that creates knots around us. Each day it fixes and we are deprived of chances and are more desperate every second as if our personal voice is being taken away.

There are people who claim to be authentic "narcissistic attractor". Why is this happening? What is the reason behind not being able look up a profile like this, and therefore not being in a position to protect ourselves from it? If we look at it all in context the kind of person attracts the most sensitive and compassionate people.

There may be a certain type of critique, in which one side is in support for the opposite. However it is important to note that there isn't any conclusive evidence on the subject due to the fact that indeed, this type of persona draws us all and pay no attention to our appearance, age or social standing. The reason for this is based on the fact that, right from the beginning the narcissists tend to be extremely attractive.

Therefore, showing characteristics such as extraordinary kindness, enthusiasm, robust comical bent and a sense of humor, and a sparkling extraversion that will never go unnoticed is normal of these. But, beneath that glistening streak is the real skin that is distinguished by the incomparable ability to create an incredibly solid connection with someone.

Relationships with narcissism. Tips on how to behave

The way that narcissism is portrayed within the relationship is related to various real-world elements. It is therefore common for two unique the kind events to occur and the second is that narcissism originates from two couples.

The other is that it is one of two that is a lawful and evident part in a lead that is equally harmful as it is to the relationship in general. There are definitely two things we need to examine.

Narcissism within the couple: when one are selfish

It is crucial to differentiate the narcissistic behavior from a character problem. In the latter instance, we'll examine a condition that is covered within the Diagnostic and Statistical Manual of Mental Disorders.

The reality of the situation could indicate that in a marriage, two people are involved in the same character type, or in this particular issue. This isn't a normal thing, however it could happen. In addition, another thing that can occur in the structure of a relationship can be described according to the following:

* We set aside the needs of our couple for our own needs.

* It's not only the ferocious disregard that comes out. Additionally, certain behaviors are evident, such as the need for control,

and the wonderful and horrible occasions where we need our companion to be with us, and at times occasions, we require to be separated.

What's the best way to explain this type of relationship? What is the result when relationship narcissism arises from two people? The result is the relationship is entangled in a pit where eventually it'll come to the point of no return. There are couples who cease to be in love but are unable to move towards an end that is safe.

A friend of mine is extremely narcissistic. what do I do?

The narcissism of the relationship is usually evident within one or the people. Therefore, it's over time that the other person becomes conscious of the real nature of the person they love. As of today, it is evident that the deep respect that was once ascribed to the person's lifestyle disappears.

Tips for evaluating and making decisions

Never question yourself. When there is a sense of narcissism within the relationship apparent, there are two options: react or accepting living in a state of complete surrender. If we choose the latter possibility, we'll end finding ourselves questioning ourselves, our confidence and self-image.

Compromised and rifts: Would they claim that they are justifiable, in spite of all the hassle? Being a narcissistic companion means being in a thrilling ride of removal and compromise. It's possible that at some point you'd have the strength to end the relationship. However the narcissist could be romantic to "capture us" time and time again. Think about what this means for your opulence.

They want you to believe in their confidence, but where are you? Narcissists aren't able to create the concept of a focussed self. In this regard, to enhance and strengthen their self-image they require someone to take over the task. Then they can rely on the other person to assert their own self-image. Consider if this is a legitimate decision, regardless of all the hassle. Think about what you'd like to be in five or ten years.

Affirmations to neutralize an Narcissist

The method to kill an egotist is to evaluate the validity of your statements or control without being distracted by the appeals you usually possess. The most important thing isn't to be afraid, since they tend to be threatening those who challenge their authority.

It's not easy to kill a narcissist to say the least. Starting with this kind of person generally is a fascinating attraction and a crucial social aid. Most of them have at least several truly captivating characteristics in their personas. They aren't usually considered to be narcissistic, but can be influenced by an magic that is a magic wand.

From the very beginning the narcissist often incites admiration to other people. We talk about the greatest messenger of his accomplishments, and they is a constant expansion of inflatables. In this regard, while for many people that"I" represents the perspective "I" is the main focus that is most narcissists have they are significantly more.

The person in question usually has a pertinence position. Assuming that this is true, then they typically rule in a highly orderly way. There are often people close to them who are devoted to them, which makes it extremely difficult to stand against them. There ways to counteract an egotist, and doing it is less difficult than you might think. It is a matter of character and capabilities. What about taking look at five statements that establish cutoff points for these kinds of individuals.

1."No," the magic word to neutralize the narcissist

The narcissist is always required to be heard to "yes." Others must help to see your views to be their own. Being able to get others to accept your actions or words is a sign of control. It means that your influence or influence on others is not questioned.

"No" is among the methods to defeat an egotist. Being untrue or getting rid of the ideas you think about will definitely affect your perception of us. This is why we are in the group of blindness because we don't have the ability to see the reality.

2. I don't believe in you do not prove what you are affirming

Narcissists often lie and take various forms; many times because of situations or people increase or reduce. There are many occasions when they intentionally create situations that do not their own self-esteem, they may choose to denigrate other people, or create fantasies about themselves.

If you have a relationship with an egotist and realize that they're lying, don't spend a minute looking over their claims. Ask them to demonstrate or prove what they've stated. Make the arguments that challenge the validity of their statements. They'll likely react by dissociating themselves. But, they'll also realize that you're not going to believe every word they say as if they were absurd.

3. You are nothing less, or more than anyone else.

In all likelihood the narcissist is not at ease to think about proving that they are superior than other people. So, it's common for them to try to claim that they know more, are better in some way, or think differently or perform better than others.

It is important to remind the person that although they may be able to perform something, for instance, or think about things more easily than others, it does not make them superior to anyone else.

It is important to stress that anyone can, with the right preparation or under the right conditions, is able to surpass expectations in any area. Also, insist on the manner in which it's possible for a person to be dominant in one aspect, and being second rate in another because this is the norm for each individual.

4. I'm not scared

The best way to eliminate a narcissist isn't to be scared of them. They base their power on the insanity and fears of other people.

Someone who is extremely aware of the weaknesses of others and attacks precisely the areas that hurt. It's acceptable to discuss the flaws of others, and even use embarrassing actions to make others uneasy.

Refraining from assaults is a way of showing that you're not afraid. The person is able to disapprove as they want. Refraining from letting your rage influence you is a unique way to get rid of an egotist. They don't think about how to behave with someone who doesn't seem to be apprehensive of their behavior.

5. Don't alter the subject

The narcissist is always required to get rid of it. If they are examining a topic and become lost and lose focus, they'll change the topic and refrain from motivating the next. If they make a mistake in their actions, they'll try to divert your attention to a different area. They're usually extremely adept in these areas.

If you have a conversation with a narcissist, or have to handle someone who is such as that, it's important to be prepared to prevent your attention from straying off the topic and wrapping up. Gather around on the inside reason for the discussion. Revert back to the main issue. In all likelihood you will not admit to their error, but will recognize that they are unable to take control of you.

The process of removing a narcissist from your life isn' by any means. It requires understanding, courage and energy. The goal of this capability isn't just to let you be in the midst of chaos and help you recover binds with other people.

The issue with narcissists is that, as it turns out they don't love themselves. But, despite not letting them know they rely on other people. Do not allow them to do this to you.

Evidence of Gaslighting in Narcissistic Relationships

What can you do to determine if you've been a victim of gaslighting? What are the signs of this destructive control and mold strategy in the course of time? The answer to these questions is crucial in order to safeguard yourself from the brutal narcissism of the narcissist and begin to recover that is crucial and, as we will discuss in the future, to cut off any contact with the person who uses this kind of mental and emotional control. Here are ten indicators that you may have been or are an apex of gaslighting.

1. The perpetrator exploits the vulnerability and fears of the victim

The narcissist who has looked into the fears and the flaws of the victim during the time of love and adoration, will use this knowledge to make them vulnerable to being gaslighted by destroying their emotional and mental defenses and making them feel inadequate or vulnerable. For instance, on occasion that they discover an individual is unsure regarding their size, the person is likely to give negative feedback so that the person feels untrustworthy about the physical appearance.

The fear of depressing, despair and doubts are, for the most part, which are used by predators to create on the victims' minds the questions they have about themselves and their perception of reality.

2. The abuser behaves as if they are aware of the victim in full

The victimizer acts as if they are an omniscient storyteller , knowing in advance the thoughts of the casualty and how they live. They do not make any excuses regarding their casualty, and their choices are always unambiguous. The narcissist is skilled in marking their victim and then exposing their actions. If the casualty tries to protect themselves, or contradicts the narcissist and the narcissist claims that the victim is lying or is self-deluding.

Sometimes, the narcissist will adopt a paternalistic or defiant attitude, as if they were worried about the health and well-being of the person they are referring to or were aware, not speaking with the victim to know what they want.

3. The perpetrator will try to convince the victim that the current circumstances are "normal" circumstances, but they actually, do not.

The narcissist will try to convince the casualty that their involvement in the way they conduct their relationships with them is completely normal and acceptable, and the victim must accept that. In the event that it is fundamental that is not the case, the narcissist may present certain instances to show that their assertions are true.

It is evident that their goal is to force the victim to believe that they are "ordinary" brutally oppressive conditions. For example, in spite of "quiet treatment" they'll say that in all relationships there are "hushes," and will accuse the victim of not being able to understand or helping them to be quiet. This "standardizes" an escapist tactic as harmful and controlling in the same way as "quiet treatments."

4. The abuser will question the credibility or the judgment of the victim

If the victim responds to the situation of abuse they are subjected to the narcissist will not just dismiss it as a matter of fact, but employ it to get the victim to acknowledge that they've been unable to maintain their psychological equilibrium or their first. The narcissist might claim that the victim is tense or overly sensitive or too reliant, or are not balanced, or that they're extremely dependent, and so on.

Each of these articulations are extremely negative impact on the individual that is being questioned, will make them believe that the problem lies with their own perception as well as their ability to discern.

5. The perpetrator causes the victim to doubt themselves

The narcissist, by force of attacking the person at issue and discrediting their understanding of the reality and their own, causes the victim to begin to question their choices regarding the world and even their abilities.

After a time the victim turns into an uneasy and defiant person who is constantly seeking the support of the person who abused them.

6. The perpetrator, in light of the facts of the victim's situation is able to recall only the facts of the victim.

The narcissist will deny a few facts and statements made previously. They might claim, for example that the mastermind arrangement occurred at a different moment in relation to the one that was agreed upon, prompting the person who was injured to acknowledge that they're in error or to believe that they got it right. If the casualty tries to deny it with no proof the narcissist is dissatisfied with their statement. This causes disarray for the person who suffers.

Another kind of memories is "overlooking" of significant dates, such as birthday celebrations, celebrations and so on. Instead, the narcissist utterly recalls the mistakes and disappointments caused by the casualty at another time and liberates them by removing them off the table.

7. The victim is forced to lie to keep from a confrontation with the perpetrator

Even though they don't possess the capacity to lie due to the pressure they feel it is likely that they believe they accept the perspective of the narcissist and that their view is consistent with the perception of the Narcissist. The victim will hide information in fear that the perpetrator could use against them.

The victim is able to stay away from confronting the attacker as every encounter on their confidence and self-confidence which then sinks them further into the dark nightmare of abuse.

8. The victim is afraid to talk with others what they are experiencing, thus separating themselves from others.

The whole process of intense and mental breakdown caused by gaslighting can cause the victim to lose confidence in their fellows completely and they'll in general withdraw themselves from others and never share with others the issues they're experiencing.

In most cases, it's the narcissist that has deliberately to advance this disengagement and cut off possible bonds of family and friendship which could provide an emotional and psychological support to their victim.

9. The victim may question their own mental and emotional health.

Gaslighting ends its vicious curve as the victims themselves begin to doubt their psychological health and their enthusiastic egalization. The indoctrination that the victim of gaslighting endured has profoundly altered the perception they hold of themselves, and has made them surrender to the sway of the narcissist who is a liar.

The perpetrator has accomplished their aim in the form of total passion and mental destruction of the victim.

10. The victim shows a depressive image

As a result as a final result, the person experiences the various manifestations of melancholy, including apathy or lack of enthusiasm and sadness, thoughts of dejection and surrender, emptyness, crying at the sight of a mirror and more.

The individual is unable to react, loses vitality and becomes dull and numb.

The Best Way to Build Self-Esteem following the relationship with a Narcissist

Concerning restoring confidence after a relationship with a narcissist. All is needed are self-care and confidence. Take action to heal the hurts and restore confidence

What can I do to improve my self-confidence after a relationship with the Narcissist? This is a question many people ask themselves. They answer this by observing the outcomes that remain after a period of frustration and an ongoing blacklist. Thus, what needs to be understood in any instance is that this art of rehabilitation and mending isn't an easy process.

There are those who have been through years with an egoist. A close look at this depicts, for example that at some point in moment, the person is able to look up, recognizing certain thoughts that they'd previously ignored. The first one is that being around these people can be harmful. The second is that there's usually an extensive period that you're completely aware that the most ideal thing to do is to end the connection. However, the heart isn't be trusted; it's an amazing paste fueled by dread.

There are many people who fear closure because they don't have any idea of how the narcissist would react. It is also normal to get caught in the bounce back effect; that is, to end the relationship only to begin it again. It's a way through and back, and even though we are assured that certain perspectives and practices will not be repeated the same mental tenets are repeated with the same exclusion.

The act of leaving a narcissist can be an act of desperation as well as courage and health. However, following the separation, a major stage begins the process of remaking since some time ago, mismanaged confidence.

"An an egotistical person is one who wants to talk about themselves even when you're not even able to teach them about themselves."

- Jean Cocteau

How can I rebuild my self-esteem after a relationship with an egotist

Broken bones recuperate. The ailment, the smudges and scraping are treated with a reasonable amount of consideration within half one month. However, injuries to the tissues of confidence, of self-image, individual qualities, or even character, aren't healed by betadine or anti-infection medications or with the passage of time.

To regain my confidence after my relationship with the narcissist I require a solid plan of action. It's not enough to let the time go by in light the fact that if something happens is happening, the gap will remain there and we'll in the end be thinking about the influence that we've been subjected to. There is no way to regain satisfaction without confidence being reclaimed, due to the fact that the mental ability is the only thing that can be tied to every aspect.

In this regard How about we look at the keys that can help us in reconstructing the scene.

Chapter 8: Finding Emotional Release

There are a lot of emotions throughout and after the end of a relationship that is abusive. Gaslighting is a traumatic form of abuse. The effects on your mental health could be overwhelming. However, this doesn't mean you should continue getting caught up in the whirlwind of emotions. It is possible to lessen your load and provide the emotional freedom that you've always wanted. There's no reason to remain trapped in this state of mind for a long time. This is the reason this chapter is all about letting go. There will be emotions but let them them go is what will allow you to get over the negative thoughts that has taken over your life. This chapter also serves as an all-encompassing tool to let your emotions take center stage. You are welcome to revisit these tips and exercises anytime your emotions have been wreaking destruction on your life. They're meant to be utilized again and time again since everyone experiences emotions and everybody should understand what works best for them when they express their feelings.

Tips to let your emotions go

1. Ride the Emotional Rollercoaster

It's okay to be in your feelings for a time. Allow yourself to feel the emotion as intensely as you can. Allow it to take over for a few days. Feelings are good, but being unable to experience them is a risk. This is because you're denying parts of yourself and are too similar to the way you lived in the past when you felt slighted. If you're unhappy, you can sad for a long time. You can go through a whole box of tissues if have to. It is likely that letting your body take over for a time can leave you exhausted that there isn't space left to continue crying. This is the reason. Allow the feeling to develop, and then put it aside. A few days is the maximum amount you could dwell on a sensation. Then, you're clinging to it too much and you could end up stuck on the same loop. Go on a rollercoaster of emotions, be aware that you must leave.

2. Breathe In Breathe Out, Breathe In

The simple word is incredibly effective. You might feel a bit dumb or uncomfortable sitting there breath in, out but there's ample research to show how easy breathing exercises can ease the tension in your body and your mind. It is relaxing your nervous system which allows you to let go of emotions that were clogging your body and dragging you down. There is no need to think of a way to do it. There are many videos on breathing exercises, and you can also check out meditation classes. Meditation classes can be extremely useful since they typically combine breathing exercises and contemplation exercises. If you take this practice every week, it can be an integral element of your routine. It's also a good method of letting your feelings know that it's time to let go. Breathing helps you get from the rut in being in a loop of emotions. It is not necessary to go through the same cycle of stress, anger and anxiety in a continuous loop. Take a few deep breaths. Allow your breathing to reset your both your mind and body.

3. Retreat

It's totally acceptable to let your life go for a few days. Consider it as taking yourself on a retreat. The goal isn't to enter "vacation state" but rather to give yourself an opportunity to release yourself from the stressors you're storing up. If you allow yourself to be in the opportunity to experience a different environment, with new people and a brand new "normal" for some time and you might be being able to find the clarity and peace in a way that you can't even if you were at home. Sometimes, leaving the world to the side could be all you need to do to offer you a new outlook of your life. When deciding where to go on a retreat look for locations that do not focus on having a fast pace. That's not the point for a spiritual retreat like this. You're seeking a location where you can relax and relax. This may look different for different individuals. While you shouldn't always be on the move but it's fine to include some things that help you feel the feeling of calm. For some, this could be an ocean. For others, it could be an area of forest. Others, it could be an international spot or a tranquil village. It is essential to select a spot that you won't be distracted by the recollection of your past. You should pick a location that is unique and exclusive to you.

4. Plug Into New Outlets

Every person has a set of emotional outlets that they have relied upon over the decades. These are your habits of emotional expression that you rely on as the emotions start to overtake you. For certain people, these avenues are beneficial and beneficial. For others, they can be harmful. The likelihood is that you'll need to rebuild and reset your emotional channels. If you've been slighted by your parents, you've probably been taught to suppress and hide emotions until you melt or until it is a part of what you feel. This is a harmful and dangerous habit. There is no need to have an emotionally explosive bomb on the verge of to explode, or an emotional hoarder. It is time to search for better and healthier outlets to connect to. An excellent example is exercise. It's not for everyone, in all likelihood, but moving your body produces chemical reactions to your body. The chemical effects are altering your brain's state of mind and emotional equilibrium to your advantage. If you're unsure to start, you should at least try to experiment with a new type of exercise, or enroll in some guided classes. A lot of people are more successful when they establish an exercise routine when they've already invested in classes. This is a good method of ensuring that you are accountable since you don't wish to let your money be wasted.

5. Tap Into Your Creativity

It is possible to resist this method because you don't consider yourself as a person who is creative. The purpose of this tip isn't to become the next celebrity artist however. You can even make something that you can throw to the side if you wish. The key to creative thinking for you can be found in the way you work. You can explore your emotions while drawing or paint, dance or perform. You can create an art piece where you throw the paint around, throw the paint and rub it around by using your hands. You can choose colors, patterns that make you feel as if they are a reflection of your mood at the moment. Put it all on the canvas , or in your dance moves , or with the expressions you choose to use to portray a character. Perhaps you'd like to write your own character, and give advice to the character. The possibilities are endless and you could not just release your feelings but also create something amazing while doing it. It's okay to mess up and have enjoyable.

6. There's no Time for Action? Try distraction

If you're struggling to let the emotion go, and there is nothing else functioning, it's ok to take a moment to divert yourself. Put the issue aside that is unsolved and then throw yourself into an activity that is demanding and time-consuming. This is the ideal moment to tackle household tasks. It will provide many advantages. If you've previously shared your space with someone else This is your chance to create a space that looks fresh and new, meaning that the experiences are less overwhelming and ever-present. Then, you'll feel more comfortable in control of your personal space. There may be a time when you don't have to confront your emotions head-on However, you are tackling something, and you are doing it right. This concrete victory can assist you in preparing for a final emotional victory. Your focus will be dependent on the accomplishments you made. Additionally, home projects can be a great way to build the strength of your mind and self-confidence. Your living space will appear like you and you'll have many of the best emotions to lean on, such as confidence and self-confidence. This will help you be more relaxed when you come back to the feelings you put aside and take on the challenge. It is a good idea to remind yourself that you've already had a great time and you can certainly do more.

7. Smile As if You Are Trying To

This exercise could cause you to laugh or cause you to roll your eyes. Try to give it a go. Take a look in the mirror. Take a look at yourself. Then smile deeply. Make sure to show that you are content. If you can't smile by yourself or even on your own, put on an amusing video or play on your smartphone and turn your head whenever you smile. The genuine joy you feel is radiating. Take a walk in the public and smile with anyone you meet. You'll be amazed by the emotion you attain just by getting back smiles from people you've never met. You're connecting with the world and people who surround you. What they see in you is happiness. Your smile can bring happiness and is an excellent way to cheer your spirits in a time when all you see is negative thoughts. Smile and be happy. Even if it doesn't work the first timearound, try again. Smiles can be infectious and you'd like to see your smile be a part of every aspect that you live.

8. Steer Free of the Past

In giving your feelings space, you could be tempted back to your victim when you reflect. It is possible to convince yourself that this is helpful or beneficial but it's not a wise choice. Consider it as a return to the scene of a horrific crime. There is no need for further reminders of the past. If you decide to reach out to the person responsible for creating the toxic past, you are exposing yourself to the same toxicity over and over again. This is not something you want to do in a moment when you're already overwhelmed. It can be the poison that keeps you in your emotional trance. The only thing from the past you're able to go back to is your former self. It's fine to engage in an internal dialogue with that part of yourself who was present before you were slighted. Be aware that part of you is from the past. You are creating an entirely new you. Your past is part of this process However, you do not need to carry your emotional baggage. Let it go.

9. Sweet Dreams

Sleep is beneficial. A healthy sleeping cycle will have a major impact on the overall quality of your overall health. The body will be more relaxed. The mind is more clear. You'll have more energy and be in a better state. Your mood will have time to shut down. Sleep is a great way to hit that reset key. There's also some merit to having your sleep be a way to put a distance between yourself and your negative experiences. This doesn't mean just the experiences you have with gaslighting. Perhaps you experienced one or two failures in the past and you took several steps backwards during the healing process. As you fall asleep the next night, those mistakes have been dealt with. The next day, your aim should be to leave and perform positive actions. The negative experiences don't remain the same between days. It is possible to begin over and begin again with every new day. As you lie down, you should not think about the day that happened too long. Recognize how it made you feel and then put the incident aside. You're now ready to begin new in the morning, with a new batch of confidence to guide you towards success. Sleep is like an eraser, giving you a brand new slate. Choose what you want to write down on that slate every day.

10. You can go down the Rabbit Hole

Sometimes, our thoughts turn into obsessions. This is what we think about every day, in and out. It is a very exhausting activity and it is a workout in futility. There is nothing you can accomplish when you are chasing your thoughts around your head all day long. Instead of focusing in a futile pursuit, channel it to use in something different. Choose a topic you enjoy. Maybe it's an area of literature that you enjoy reading. Maybe it's a novel of new recipes you'd like to cook. Perhaps it's adorable cat videos. Whatever it is, just sit down and be fascinated by the topic. Learn to be an expert in love stories. Learn to become a pastry chef in the kitchen of your own. Check out a selection of cute cat videos and attempt to make your own. Make it something you are able to engage in all ways. Join forums that discuss the topic or read books on the subject and join groups whenever you are able to. You'll not only be getting away from your thoughts, but also be attracted by something positive or enjoyable. The pursuit doesn't have to be an "point" apart from it is a source of joy. This kind of thing can give you hours, days, weeks or even decades of pleasure. It will also bring you closer to others who share your interests, which will boost your enjoyment and perhaps your social network.

Chapter 9: Self-Consciousness A Plan for Dealing With Emotional Manipulators

The term "self-consciousness" is often understood as a sign of being uncomfortable with yourself and anxious about the negative reaction of others. It's usually thought of as an over-focused awareness of us and what others think of our perception of ourselves. If you break it down into its original philosophical or psychological meaning, it's not so bad because it translates to an increased awareness of oneself. It's the ability to reflection, the ability to examine ourselves and discover our true nature. With a greater sense of self-awareness, comes the ability to comprehend your own thoughts, feelings behaviors, motives, and behaviours. Anyone who has reached this self-awareness isn't a tool for manipulators of emotions. They recognize that you can't be played with.

Self-consciousness is a crucial part of your total emotional intelligence approach when confronting manipulators. The first step is becoming aware of and identify your feelings. When you are conscious of what you feel at any moment, no one is able to bring your feelings back at you as a method of manipulation techniques. You could be experiencing a low moment in your life due to having a very bitter breakup or divorce. Feelings such as anger, sadness, loneliness and even shock are sparked during this time. This is the time of year that you're extremely susceptible to manipulation by emotional people. They can appear attractive at first, while doing the right things. They're all working toward winning your love. They're like a goal to them. When you get caught up in their pranks, you're an instrument for them. They can then mold you into whatever they want. The increased self-consciousness will expose your vulnerability before others detect the scent. This way, you'll be able to fight away from their tactics.

The self-consciousness approach can aid in identifying your thoughts and the thoughts that go through your head. Self-defeating thoughts are uncovered and exposed. Self-critical self-talk is also examined. After being identified the steps taken are to remove the negative thoughts that are a part of your brain. The manipulators of emotions have characteristics like the ability to "read" individuals, making them extremely dangerous. They will be able to spot your self-esteem issues and utilize to push you down. It's a way to gain power for them. They're looking to control you and even the smallest hint that they receive about your vulnerability can make you a target for them.

Self-consciousness can increase your sense of sense of intuition. We all have this instinctual sense of intuition. It is a feeling that things don't seem right in certain situations. Self-conscious individuals have this intuitional sense that is extremely high. People who manipulate emotions can tell whether people are on their side. Your intuition can act as a warning signal for them. This way, they can be left alone and look for their next prey. Your highly intuitive level could also act as a guide for identifying the manipulators. So, you'll be able to accept their direct responses and give them no chance to evade concerns. When you find an issue, you can identify them and pressure them to acknowledge their responsibilities.

Self-consciousness is a method that can be used to stop manipulators. If you have a spouse who are emotionally manipulative must use this technique frequently. It helps keep their heads above the water and makes sure they do not get overtaken by the plethora of problems that could arise in the course of a relationship.

Chapter 10: Top Red Flags To Indicate You're Being Mistreated

If you've ever been around a colleague, friend or partner who's a psychopath suffering with NPD (narcissist personality disorder) this is a sign that you were the victim of gaslighting. Like we said earlier it is a manipulative technique used by narcissists in order to cause harm to their victim. Gaslighting is a technique used by narcissists to trigger a reaction regardless of whether it's anger, frustration or even sadness. They're trying to trigger an emotional response from you. They would like you to feel unsecure They would like you to feel guilty. Therefore, they attempt to make you feel as if your feelings are not normal and not rational. They can make you question yourself because they want get you to feel like a crazy person since they make it seem like the way you react to their abuse isn't rational.

It will be difficult to describe the situation as it was because, the moment you became involved, you weren't able to understand the circumstances. If you have a relationship with a narcissist for more than two months, you'll be aware that you've made a big mistake. If you feel that you're a of a freak and not able recognize the issue, even though the situation is occurring because it helps you handle the situation better, then it is a sign that you're being gaslighted. Understanding how to recognize signs that indicate you are being gaslighted can help you live a better.

If you're aware of the actions that lead an egotist to engage in gaslighting and snarking, you'll be able respond differently and alter the course of action.

Your worries are being made use of against you

The first indication is that your anxieties are being made to work against you. This means that narcissists can be charming, in their very own unique way. Sometimes, they'll take in every word you speak, and attempt to highlight the weaknesses that you have shared with them to make them feel worse about them. For example, if, for instance, you have told someone a narcissist you feel unsecure regarding how much weight you weigh, then the individual will make a sly assertion regarding your weight.

If you're involved in a relationship that is romantically committed to this person, he could even make remarks about people who are more attractive than you. If you tell them that you're overweight, they will discuss other women. If you complain that you're thin, they'll talk about thinner women. If you make a complaint to the narcissist in your life they'll talk about things that are completely opposite to the issue, so that you're feeling uneasy about your own self. Gaslighters usually exploit your anxieties. Narcissists have a primary purpose, that will make you question your own self so that you become dependent on him.

You don't have your mind.

Another indication that you're being gaslighted is that you aren't in what you think in your head. Narcissists may claim to be aware of the thoughts of their mind and assert the opposite. They don't wish others thinking the same thing. If you refuse to are thinking what you think they'll say you're lying. In the extreme instances they'll inform you that you're lying and claim that you are lying since as a narcissist they cannot be lying even when thoughts are going through your head.

You don't even know what's normal

Another indication that you're being gaslighted is the fact that you don't know what's normal. If you're being informed that things are normal, but deep inside of you, you realize that they're not This means that you're a person who has been gaslighted. If, for instance, your boss says that you need to tell a client that you are lying about the safety of an product you plan to offer the item, and you claim that this isn't ethical. Your boss will then declare that all employees lie on behalf their employers. If you aren't a team player , perhaps you should consider a new job.

Similar things can happen in a marriage when one man has a self-destructing wife. In this case, the woman who is a narcissist might ask that "hey could you tell our children lies and say that I've spent my dinner money on something else. If the husband doesn't say yes she will ask, "why can't you lie for me? The truth is that all husbands lie to their wives. They are constantly telling them things and telling you that everyone else does it , so why wouldn't you take it on.

The diagnosis was made by Narcissists

The next thing to consider is when you're diagnosed with a serious issue and not by a medical professional however by an person who is a narcissist. When a narcissist appears to be lying or attempting to manipulate you or a coworker, who isn't getting their way, they'll intensify the situation by posing questions about your sanity. He could call you insane. He could call you sensitive. He might inform you that you require therapy. It's all about controlling yourself and not a lot other than that. A narcissist does not really care if the words he's using hurt you. He's amused by it. The person who is narcissist doesn't think about the fact that what he says hurts you, and he's amused by the situation. They'll even accuse their children of stealing what they want.

If you are unsure about your beliefs and beliefs

Next, you must decide to question your beliefs and assumptions. He'll inform you that the things you believe isn't the truth. For instance, if you've got an apathetic mother, she'll claim that your partner is a huge fat loser and you must eliminate him. After a while you'll begin to believe that and could end up damaging your relationship with the person, because you doubted your own judgement. Therefore, you must be able to trust yourself. It's impossible to recall anything any longer.

Additionally, the person who is a narcissist is extremely good at keeping his inexhaustible memory. They'll claim that they never did something that upsets you in particular if they said some thing like "hey I'm upset by you." They'll say it even when you confront them objectively about the issue. Sometimes, they'll claim that "you are just a bit of rubbish." When you look them in the eye and say, "did you really say that I'm a piece rubbish?" they'll say"no, I didn't say anything like that." Even if you recorded them in a recorded conversation saying something, they'll insist that they didn't intend to say that in a negative way.

The point is that they deny the bad behavior and at times, they assure you that they will take a different approach but they don't actually perform it. Sometimes they may admit that they didn't need to say however, in the future, they'll refuse to admit it. Narcissists use clever language to justify his actions and act like his actions are perfectly normal.

They'll appear like your actions are not rational.

Incessantly lying to keep the peace

Another sign that you're being gaslighted is when you lie to maintain the peace. This happens the moment you tell yourself that you do not want any other individuals in your life. Because of the immense stress this person has put over you, you'll discover that you are lying. You'll be bending the truth to the narcissist in order to avoid physical and verbal violence that will be the outcome of any discussion. the narcissist is not acceptable against any of his standards.

Try to look hot

The second sign that you're getting gassed is are trying to appear hot. This is a major warning because, as human beings we are conditioned to share our thoughts and experiences with others. our thoughts with those who are in our lives. If you're dealing with someone who is a narcissist and you see a sign that you're being slighted and you are. are talking about yourself. Then, you begin talking about the person, and then you'll begin to rely on the extent of your relationship with that individual. You may even quit talking about yourself completely. It's not wise to let this go on since if one day you're out there and someone asks you a questions about you and you'll get stuck. You will not be able to speak about yourself any more.

It isn't even a good idea to discuss yourself because you're so unsure due to the abuse that the narcissist forced you to endure. It is important to recognize more than the narcissist wants you to think that you're insane. The narcissist's ferocity manipulative tactics and manipulation can take hold of you, and when you realize that, you'll look for a solution to settle the dispute now. You'll end up convincing yourself the person who is narcissistic has the right idea and that there are some things you could do better. You'll tell yourself that the behavior of the narcissist is a reaction to your errors. Then you will begin to believe that you're the one to blame and will begin apologize to the person who is a narcissist. If you do make an apology to the narcissist, he will likely accept your apology and afterwards, he'll mention the bad behaviour that you apologized for in your face.

Depression

Another sign that you're being deceived is depression. If the narcissist is able to wear you down, you'll be always anxious and depressed. you'll constantly doubt yourself due to your despair. You'll feel exhausted from the rollercoaster ride that the Narcissist has taken you on. It is possible that you're a too sensitive due to the manipulative tactics you are subjected to. This is why you become confused and start feeling lost. You are more likely to seek assistance with depression than the real issue that is the gaslighted way of life. Even the regular relationships that you have with your loved ones could be impacted by miscommunications or miscommunications. When someone begins using manipulative tactics of gaslighting you, chances are the person may be a Narcissist. If you're looking to stop the behavior of this person, you must to alter the way you live my life.

Chapter 11: Gaslighting Friends Are My Friends Gaslighting Me?

It's difficult to comprehend that our most beloved friends are geared up to manipulate us in ways we would never imagine. One extremely risky form of this control is called gaslighting. In close relationships gaslighting can mean disgracing someone for their actions and separating the disgrace to reinforce it with no trust in alleviation. It is often difficult to discern gaslighting when you're in a relationship however it's possible, and it's important. To aid in deciphering gaslighting, must take your time and pay attention to your body's signals, remember the characteristics that a real relationship likes, try to understand your flaws (as gaslighters see them) and then consult an expert for assistance. It is said that your companions are the people you choose to be with. There is no need to spend every ounce of energy in them, but you should enjoy each other's conversations and you support one another through triumphs and unfortunate events; you really get the best of each other. If nothing else it's the one thing we'd like to see in a friend... in reality the people we love can fool us. Furthermore, they are able to employ a specific method of control to obtain what they want from the relationship.

How can you spot gaslighting within Close Friendships?

The reality is that the people closest to us are the ones who are at hand to gaslight us, as this kind of control thrives on proximity. If you're not familiar by the term gaslighting, it is the act of influencing someone, using mental techniques, to question their own rationality as well as their own intuition, reality, and instinct. People who engage in it are doing it for personal focus and are often an egocentric character. In addition, one would not think of a friend as gaslighting them, but it is a common occurrence. Jor-El Caraballo is a medical professional and co-creator for

Viva Wellness, clarifies what gaslighting can look like in relationship:

"Gaslighting is a way of shaming and forcing someone to be smug or apathetic. It's usually about the person who is trying to the control. In close relationships as well as fellowships and close connections, you'll witness an instance of discrediting someone's actions and possibly also segregating the person from any power that might increase their worth or promote certainties (e.g. the separation of an the individual from other friends and family members who can articulate the reality of things or view them more clearly)."

Why is this happening?

There and then The person doing the gaslighting isn't aware of it. Sometimes it's something related to the own flaws in being off base or being less powerful in relationships. The uncertainties can cause conflicts as teenagers or from previous relationships. However, on contrary it could be the kinds of weaknesses which we struggle to overcome - it can be a challenge to be difficult to admit when you're in error. In a variety of situations this could be a deliberate tactic to make the person's friend feel less confident and less likely to take on the challenge. It is a completely unsatisfactory act and is a particularly brutal example of behavior.

Beware of Your Gaslighting Friends Five Tips To Avoid Gaslighting

Because we don't believe that our closest friends to manipulate us in this manner that it is much more difficult to identify gaslighting behaviour in our friends, but it's important that we recognize it. Here are some professional tips to recognize and overcoming the influence of a friend:

1.) Start slowly.

"When you realize what's going on I counsel my patients to take a step back and cautiously in trying to escape the situation," says Psychiatrist Dion Metzger, MD. "Trust with a trusted friend and realize that you might have to perform a penance in order to end this relationship.

Consider your emotional health as an imperative and be aware that the penance will eventually be justified, despite all the hassle."

2.) Pay attention to the body language.

Julie Williamson, an authorized expert advocate, suggests that you must be aware of your perception of the person being mentioned: "Somebody can safeguard against gaslighting by being aware of the things they're experiencing in their body and also what their brain is trying to let them know. If something happens, and they think that the other person will try to convince they didn't cause it by recording the event, along with the time and date will provide an update of what they saw during the incident."

3.) Be aware of what real friendship is like.

It is important to be aware of what a true and private relationship looks like. "Shielding yourself from being gaslighted requires you to be able to discern the signs of manipulation through being aware of the risks," says Sheri Heller an authorized clinical social specialist. "Try not to get influenced by axioms or prizes. Be realistic about what real friendship and closeness resemble. The process of trusting requires time and defenselessness that is anchored and adjusted. Being able to feel a sense of self-assurance and confidence in your own self-recognizances ensures that the deceit of the abuser who stealthy grasp hold."

4.) Plug in the gaslighter in your body.

Award Brenner is a therapist and co-creator of the Relationship Sanity program:

Building and Maintaining Healthy Relationships It is important to recognize your flaws, as gaslighters see the following: "Perhaps the most ideal method to combat gaslighting is to come close to your inner gaslighter. The human race is a master of fraud, and self-double dealing. In the event that we discover our weaknesses and triggers, as well as our own personal triggers and relationships, as well as the ways we respond internally, we are stronger against gaslighters and other work threats to our environment."

5) Ask a professional.

Finally, in the event you're not certain about a particular relationship or you require a little guidance, consider talking with an expert in emotional wellbeing. "At the point where you begin to feel that you're getting insane (on the basis that a gaslighter has made you feel like that) be sure to consult for help from a professional. Talk to a professional to get fresh eyes on the situation since your companions may be, in certain instances, be biased in their opinions," says Kim Chronister, PsyD, an authorized clinical psychologist.

The words used by toxic friends

Here are some common gaslighting words that can come from a toxic person:

"I was just kidding!"

It could have felt like they were laughing however, it's all fine today, right? They just claimed they were joking, therefore it's not it's a huge deal... It's okay. Sure.

"You mentioned that you were going to go to an action film on Saturday. Did you forget?"

It's something I've observed gaslighters do to friends in situations where they're losing control of you. You've never stated that you want to see the cinema They know this too, yet they'd like to think of something that makes you feel guilty for them. You now have to pay them for your time which was never ever even offered in the first place. It's not your obligation to them If someone were to make you feel like a slur then you probably would not have had the intention of spending time with them in the first instance.

"I only have a problem with you because I am in love with you."

I've heard it a lot and it's a highly extremely sly gaslighting expression. If you're one the "mean people" who are critical of your every move This isn't as nice as they believe it to be. It's not even fun If it is hurtful to you emotionally and reduces the self-esteem of yours. This is a sly way of saying it since they are able to add an element that says they're very close to you, and are only trying to make you feel bad because "that's the best thing to you."

"Is you experiencing a problem in your life?"

In time, this harmful friendship is likely to be a source of irritation and that's why you become frustrated and angry after many occasions of them being manipulative. There is probably something wrong with your character, it's likely that you didn't get enough sleep or did you? There's no problem with your. Being the victim of this type of manipulation is a sigh of relief, and getting rid of it can be more difficult because the gaslighter may use more manipulative words for convincing you they aren't the issue, but you are.

"I'm just like everyone else Do not take it personally."

Perhaps they may be, but if what you've heard from them feels like it's taking them over the top and isn't acceptable, they should be punished. If your friend continues to engage in this kind of behavior, regardless of the amount of time you've spent with them you should end their relationship. Someone who is draining you and frequently makes you doubt your own sanity isn't one you should having around. If you're with a person such as this, make sure you take your time with what they're saying, and get them out of the way.

What Do You To Do If You Could be a Gaslighter?

It's extremely brave and self-aware of your first step of admitting that you might be having problems. It's not an easy task. Changes to abusive behaviors that are ingrained is challenging, but it is possible to be accomplished. Most often, the abusers were victims by their own family members, or experienced other traumatizing experiences which they are trying to take control of to turn them into victims instead of seeking safe outlets.

One thing to look into is consulting an experienced therapist who is specialized in issues of domestic violence for men or joining an men's support group.

These are some suggestions for the ways that those who abuse or harass women must do in order to alter their behavior:

Acknowledge the things you've done

Stop rationalizing and thinking

Compensation is due.

Accept responsibility and accept that the mistreatment of others is not a random act.

Find patterns of control behavior you are using

Find the arrogances that start your deceit

Don't give excuses (ex. "I haven't had a similar experience to this for quite a while so it's nothing except a huge ordeal)

Develop mindful and kind, solid habits

Make a change in how you respond in response to the partner's (or the previous partner's) anger and complaints

Make changes to how you conduct yourself in disputes

Accept whatever consequences you incur from what you do (including not getting angry over the outcomes and not blaming your children or partner of being guilty)

What steps can you decide to take?

If you are able to identify yourself as being in any of the above situations, you should investigate the triggers within yourself, possibly with the help of a professional. Even a mild gaslight is a sign of a serious issue that you're not addressing or a desire to make other people feel inferior in order to feel good about yourself. A well-prepared advisor can help in analyzing this. The aim should be to get to an area where you are able to actively feel, and then be able to express your thoughts regarding your companion. Conversations should revolve around appreciating and empathizing to her thoughts instead of imposing or making a choice about the issues. Your relationship will prove to be more solid, as will you.

Chapter 12: Exposing Abusive Conduct

You'll have disputes with your partner every once in a while; it's not a big deal. This is how relationships function. In a relationship that's healthy and you're both happy, you'll go your individual ways, relax slightly, and then work to make things better together.

But, if your arguments begin to escalate into violence and you begin to feel a sense of resentment, this is not normal. You can tell whenever you and your spouse begin to behave with the intention of controlling or dominate you (or someone else) either physically or psychologically. There's a temptation to try to hide emotional abuse with the excuse, "Well, they never struck my body, therefore I'm fine." But, abuse is always the norm and is not okay. This isn't because of your fault or that you're flawed in any way. Remember that!

The Problem with emotional Abuse

The issue of emotional abuse is, since it doesn't leave marks that it is not visible, and often is ignored or is nearly impossible to detect when it occurs. It is important to remember that the impact of emotional abuse is extremely real, and will last for a very prolonged duration.

If you're being psychologically abused and the person who is abused is making statements and actions to influence you to think what they'd like. The aim is generally to leave you confused or disillusioned and completely dependent on them to provide your self-esteem and self-worth. It's a very horrible, degrading act to commit to another person and could lead to real mental health problems like depression, post-traumatic stress Disorder and anxiety.

Unmasking Emotional Abuse

There are numerous misconceptions about emotional abuse that do a great job of concealing the issue to make it difficult to recognize. Let's take off the mask and be more confident in figuring out if someone you love is being victimized.

Myth #1: Physical abuse is usually followed by physical assault.

It's not. It is possible to experience emotional abuse that is not physical violence; however, this usually isn't noticed.

Myth #2: The emotional impact of abuse isn't nearly as destructive like physical violence. This is simply a lie. If it causes pain, it does. It's not an effective argument to claim that one kind of abuse is more harmful than the other. The abuse isn't acceptable. If you're being victimized by someone else, you are deserving of betterand require all the help you are able to get.

Myth #3: The idea that emotional abuse is only a problem for women. It can affect men and women. It's not a different case. Additionally, it occurs in various other settings besides relationships, for instance at work, or with friends too.

What Should You Do If You're Being Abusive

If you're emotionally damaged and constantly criticized for what you say and do. Every day, you're blamed regardless of what can not be your responsibility. Then you're forced to become embarrassed. The gaslighter is constantly threatening to harm you physically or do something that they are sure you don't would like them to do. You feel as if you're in complete control of your life, because the person who is abusive takes the power from you, even taking control of your finances to ensure you are forced to choose other than to follow them and do what they'd like.

If you identify yourself in the above paragraph You must take action. It is time to get in touch and seek assistance. There's no shame in asking for help. In reality seeking assistance is among the most brave things you could ever do, especially if you're in a position where you've been completely worn down and beaten by the perpetrator.

Ask for assistance. It's fine to talk about your feelings with others. You'll need someone to give you the feeling of being validated. It is important to find someone who will aid you in working through what you've been through so that you can be sure for the fact that you're not insane. It is important to find someone who will provide you with hope that your life can be better. If you need counseling, check out https://www.crisistextline.org/get-help/emotional-abuse. You can also text HELLO by text message to the number 741741, and be instantly connected to counsellors who will assist you. Be safe. If the person who abuses you in your life has an habit of sifting over your cell phone make sure to delete any messages you make them.

Discuss with anyone you can about the issues you're experiencing. Trust them and you will not only have someone to rely on and support you, but you'll also be able spend your time with people other than your abusive partner. Try to find more people to meet with who will help you.

A safety plan should be put in place. Although there's no need to worry about physical violence going on, in addition to an emotional assault, it's vital to be protected. That means you must make plans on ways to escape the relationship when you're at last ready to get rid of the abuser.

Don't make excuses for the abuse

The majority times people will rely on mental illnesses to justify whatever they choose to do. They don't discuss it as if they are trying to see real change. It's a way for them to continue to treat you the same way as they have always done.

It's not unusual for someone who has abused you to attempt to minimize the situation or to blame you for the motive behind why they're acting in the manner they do. It could appear that your partner doesn't understand why they behave the way they do, or is unaware of the consequences that their choices have. This is, however, simply a lie from their side. They are aware of what they're doing. The reason they're uninformed will make you less certain of your own self-confidence. And then you begin to wonder whether you're really exaggerated or deluded! I'd like to inform you that your partner who is abusive is extremely aware of how they're hurting your feelings, and they are always in control of their actions, whether they behave, whether disorderly or not. Want proof?

They'll decide when to assault you and the extent to which they can push it. One example of this is the time they make threats to harm you, but they don't. or when they assault you in ways you are unable to tell other people, since there's no evidence, and it could appear as if you're creating something from nothing.

You are the only victim but not other people. If they really had no control over their actions, wouldn't they be able to abuse all of their family members?

However, they don't are they? This is because they keep themselves in check. If they had a mental disorder, everyone else affected by it would receive similar treatment not just you.

They exacerbate their horrible behavior. When it's about being in a state of disorder, there could be changes in the individual's state of mind. But, even in these cases there's a consistentity in how they act. You may be aware that the person you abuse occasionally choose to not be abusive for a period of time. In other instances, they'll gradually increase the amount of assault as the relationship goes along. This further proves that they are able to be different or superior.

Keep in your mind that no matter if the gaslighter is suffering from a real mental health issue it is not your person to be held accountable for their actions towards you! It is it is possible for someone to suffer from a mental disorder but still not engage in controlling manipulative and controlling methods. The patient will need to recognize their problems and be willing to seek help they require. Remember that you're not responsible for the reasons they choose to behave in like they do, so you're not the solution they require. They have to take responsibility for their actions, and only they alone are the only ones who can make the first step they'll require to transform themselves.

Chapter 13: The Way to Recover from Gaslight Effect and Narcissistic Abuse

If you're the kind who trusts anyone, you put yourself in a position to be constantly injured by other people since you constantly try to show the greatest in people. You can identify people very well, once you meet someone, you instantly know the person they are, yet you'll continue to build the relationship in order to find the best of them. You'll try to discern the heart of people and their role in the way they present themselves. You will expect them to show you how they are the person you want to be. Naturally, this could cause some negative consequences and could result in you being hurt and cause others to harm you. However, there's an portion of that which is truly beautiful should be included when you interact with others.

We usually have a way to categorize people into healthy or unhealthy and unsafe for relationships. There is a portion of our society that states that if someone reveals the person they are, then you should accept it and then cut off their communication. We are all living with the belief that everybody can be one of two things: good or evil, and If they're bad and not good, then we must eliminate them from our lives. But it is important to recognize that everyone is prone to making mistakes , and it is impossible to see an individual as who they are and what they've behaved and simply take that information and create a an all-black and white image of the person. It is a constant battle to invalidate one another every day in a way that is considered to be abusive. Invalidation of emotions occurs when someone says how they are feeling and your response to their statement is it's incorrect. A good relationship may contain emotional abuse but it does not mean that it's an unhealthy relationship. Rather, it is imperative to end the relationship and not talk with them ever again. It is always best to give people an opportunity to be a part of your life.

How to stay clear of manipulating your emotions and thoughts

In this part, we will discuss those that you have in your life who may possibly be using these shady strategies against you. If you're not a specialist in manipulation or you aren't aware that you're being controlled and manipulated, this section will guide you understand the strategies that the majority of people employ to control you, in order to gain what they want out of you. What do you need to do in order to start making sure that you aren't dealing with this kind of abuse, and that you do not engage with the person. You need to be aware of whether you are being used by someone else to manipulate you to control you in order to obtain what they want from you. It is important to know those who manipulate you, not only to make sure you don't fall victim to abuse and again, but also to know the signs that you've encountered those who use manipulative behavior on you emotionally. This section will aid you learn and be aware of the tactics people use to obtain what they want from you. This section will help you understand mental and emotional abuse, and how they relate to gaslighting.

If you find yourself in the circumstance of meeting new people, it is important to discover what's going on inside you which are causing individuals to hurt you. This means that you didn't just discover what it means to be abused, but you also learned the things you have to take care of within yourself to ensure you aren't a victim of this kind of abuse. It is important to avoid engaging in violence and discover how to truly be a good friend to yourself and defend yourself.

Blame, guilt and shame

The most effective technique that emotional manipulators uses against you is guilt, the blame, and shame. They'll use phrases such as "well If you don't take this action for me, it's a sign that you don't really care regarding my needs." "Why do you not take on this task for me? allow me to perform another task for you." They'll use phrases similar to, "if you can't do this, then I'll need no one else to assist me." They will use these words to you once you've stated "no" for them. If you've told them no and they have said no, then the person will repeat the same phrases to you. This will be making you feel guilt-ridden. They'll start blaming and blame you for the reason you aren't able to do something for them.

They'll make you feel like you must give them something that you do not want to do in order they'll be content. This will be the sole way for them be content even if you've admitted that you are unable to perform the task for them, you may even have provided the most detailed explanation to why you aren't able to accomplish that task. It's the truth that there is no reason to give a long explanations of why you are unable to perform something, since any person who really likes you and respects your wishes isn't will use shame, guilt and blame you for the reason that they're not receiving what they want or on the circumstances, they're not likely to do this.

There is no one who is healthy to do this. Additionally, nobody who values you will take that action. No one who is devoted to you will take that action. If you tell them no, them, they're expected to accept the fact that you have said no. Even if you do say"no" to a healthy person they might not agree with the response or not want to hear the word "no," however, they will still have to be able to accept the fact that you're saying no, and they can move on to live their lives. Someone who is a manipulator of emotions won't do that, because they are just an adult child who has never learned to respect boundaries.

They won't accept they are not. They're just unforgiving emotional naive. If you're dealing with someone like this there is a constant risk of being slapped. There will be a myriad of things directed at you. If you're not aware that this is the way the person is acting, and you're a codependent person and are unsure of yourself and fears, you'll be forced be a victim of shame, guilt and responsibility because the person is essentially codependent also.

Narcissists are just co-dependents too; they are just filled with different things. Therefore, their happiness depends on the person who will give them the most when they need it, since they're just children. The happiness of their lives is upon your shoulders and, since you're dependent you expect everyone else to love you. You would like everyone to show your the love of their lives. You want everyone to believe that you're a good person or a nice guy So, you're going to take their happiness and turn it into a problem and do everything you can do to ensure that they are happy and you can get all the things they want. In addition, if you've got an unsatisfactory self-esteem, you'll have a lack of confidence.

It's possible to say no at first but once the person begins trying to push back, you'll concede and not be forced to say that you're not sure. You're not sure how to remain firm in your thoughts and how you feel. If you've been an unnatural way for too long and feel that you should be facing or challenging anyone, it is an enormous challenge for you. However, you must be aware that in every moment, you are evaluated. People who abuse you the most will tend be the most obstinate with you and that's something you must be aware of.

You must look at the person who is abusive as your mentor. The person who is abusing you will give you a lot of backlash and pain to teach you to continue to rise up and be a strong advocate for yourself. When you view the issue from a different perspective you may not see things so seriously. You'll be able to comprehend why someone is what they are, and you begin to see every chance you have from the abuser as an opportunity to feel love for yourself and to be in a position to defend yourself.

Then you'll have to keep practicing it on a regular basis. You'll have to practice the art of standing up for yourself in any situation. You must practice what it takes to say no and then. It is important to practice saying no without thinking about whether someone is angry at you, or whether the person tries to slap you back or attempts to use all of these tactics against your behalf or against you.

Make him give you an answer

The other is that he'll try to force you to provide an answer. A manipulator is someone who is adamant about what they want , since they are acting like children, and because they do not know that, often there is no answer as they didn't learned to respect boundaries while they were young. They want the things they want and are looking for it now. Therefore, if they want you to offer them something, they're not likely to allow you the time to consider the issue or look through your schedule and determine whether it is a good fit for you. They don't want you to consider it. They need you to give them an answer now, since that's exactly what they are looking for.

They want answers from you, because all they're looking for is an opportunity to manipulate you to be in control of any situation. They'll ask you to do something for them. If you tell them that you'd like to consider it, they'll say that they require an answer quickly. If you hear someone say that, you must probably tell the person a "No" since the person doesn't appreciate that you'll need to take some time to speak with your spouse, or to check your calendar to confirm that the request he's making of you is going to benefit you.

Now , if someone needs to travel to the airport now You can provide the person an answer today, but when you're dealing whom you are aware is a narcissist or violent, then you'll be able to see that they continue to do it constantly. Since the person doesn't wish to consider the best option for you , because what is best for you may not be pertinent to the person.

What the person really wants is to escape this situation, and that's why they need to know the solution right now.

You're aware that if you've had to deal with a child, toddler or teenager, you'll see that they are extremely self-centered and only think about themselves. This isn't any more different. The person who is a narcissist is an innocent child living within an adult physique. The emotional and mental ability of this person are infantile. However, if the person doesn't have the patience to give you time to think about the issue and then answer, the answer should be no. If you provide an "no" answer, and the person continues to be unrelenting or inflicting shame or guilt on you, then it's essential to remain determined in your no. If you attempt to provide an explanation as to the reason you gave him a no response, it may not be needed since anyone who is devoted to you and admires you must respect that you have a not.

It's not necessary to provide a lengthy explanation of the reason what you aren't able to do to help the person.

Take the Victim card

Another thing an abuser does to you is that they play victim, which is in a way akin to the shame and guilt. It makes the person feel better about the hurt they're providing you with. If you say that they are not interested and they apply all their tactics to you, and attempt to guilt you or shame on you for why they're not getting their way, they're putting themselves in a victim-blaming mindset. If they are the abuser, that's how it works for them.

The first step is guilt and then the shame, after which comes the blame. Finally, they are able to bring up the notion of victimization, in which you're the villain while they're the nice guys. They're doing all things for you, yet you do nothing for them , and this makes them feel more powerful because they are unable to accept on the burden. However, no matter how they're trying to achieve out of this mess the responsibility is the responsibility of them, not you. It is not about you. If someone notices that you're getting closer to establishing boundaries and you've stuck to the fact that there is no response and are firmly in your position, and are not going back, they will begin to retaliate against you. They will play the victim role in order to make you feel guilty for them.

If you're someone who is codependent, or you are a people pleaser or someone who is compassionate or sympathetic to the struggles that other people go through, regardless of whether you are one of them or not, you'll try to offer the person you love. If someone needs an escort and you tell them no and the person has been through the various strategies to see if it's going to affect you, then he'll look to determine whether guilt will be a factor in your decision. If it doesn't, then look to determine whether Shame will be working on you. If not, the victim will be the victim and act as if the person is doing everything for you and you, are the opposite and don't do anything for you.

This is the various levels of abuse an abusive manipulator goes through to determine which will allow them to manipulate you to get what they want from you. If the victim mindset is not effective the manipulator will begin to bargain with you. They will begin offering you the world. They'll promise you the world. They'll lie to you to test the possibility of getting what they want from you.. Playing tick for tick.

You must now realize that the person you are talking about is a sexy person and they meticulously study their victims. They are victims to any person within their lives and it's not just the one victim they are trying to be abused. There are many people around them that they are squandering. They have people who are codependent and trying to get what they want out of them. They will use their victims in specific ways to manage them and achieve what they need. An abuser now studies his victim to determine what they require in their lives, areas that they require assistance, areas in which areas you're vulnerable, and the areas where you're weak.

They know this and begin to promise that you will give them what they want, so they can get the things they want and they begin negotiations with you. It is typical when you work with an narcissist, or in the case of co-parenting with someone who is a narcissist or if you divorce one who is narcissistic, or anyone with any sort of violent behavior. In these circumstances, they're negotiations, and they're promising that they will do everything for you. The truth is that nothing they say will ever come into the ground, since whatever they tell you is likely to be revealed from this person. The reason is that they are likely provide you with reasons or excuses for why they aren't able to fulfill what they said they would.

If they do not keep their word on what they have promised you but they'll take the promise back from you. It's not about you or what you would like in any situation. The person who is so selfish.

There is nothing authentic about this person, and the things they say during their tactics is an attempt to convince you into believing that they're an honest person and will help you when you're difficult, but the truth is that that is not the reality. For you, it is very difficult to admit that you are not the only personbecause that person is convinced that they're normal, healthy, that they are concerned about you, and that they admire you, but that's not what the person really is.

They suffer from an issue with their personality and something is happening within them, which causes them to use this method on you to attempt to take advantage of you. If they are doing all of these things and are feeling that they're still not receiving what they want out of you, they'll move on to actual abuse. This happens to anyone whom you collaborate with, one you co-parent with or with someone you may be divorcing. It is at this point that they begin to bully you, they then harass you and even make fun of you and call you names. This is when the actual violence begins to occur because you've caused a problem for the child. If a child is upset, they throw objects around or cry. play around, they experience an exuberant reaction, and then they kick their feet onto the ground. But an adult isn't likely to resort to these strategies, but instead they'll resort to naming and bullying, and threatening and they'll keep doing it for quite a long period of time.

Conclusion

Gaslighting can be described as a type of psychological maltreatment. Someone who is gaslighting may attempt to convince a victim to doubt their perception of reality. The gaslighter can persuade a victim to believe that their perceptions aren't true or that they're in a state of confusion over the smallest thing. The abuser could then make their own feelings and thoughts as "the real truth." Gaslighters/narcissists can cause a lot of injuries. On the off chance that you are involved with a gaslighter/narcissist, it might have damaged you in ways that you aren't truly aware of yet. Contemplate how the gaslighter/narcissist might be affecting your perspective on yourself and your general surroundings. Like being able communicate your feelings can help you communicate with them--along with the confidence to speak up for yourself, so do expressing your feelings differently. If you're more at ease drawing, rather than speaking, you can use drawing to clarify what you're feeling. This could assist you in taking positive steps to let go of the gas. You could seek therapy or see therapy so that you are able to recover from the negative emotions and the abusive behavior.

www.ingramcontent.com/pod-product-compliance
Lightning Source LLC
Chambersburg PA
CBHW060328030426
42336CB00011B/1251